REVIEWS FOR

Back from Death's Doorstep

Benji Evans is alive but for the grace of God. His story is one of the most compelling I have known in my greater than 45 years in health care. He survived extremely severe pancreatitis. Most cases of pancreatitis are mild and many do not even require being hospitalized. However, some are so severe that survival is unusual. Benji's was in that category. There are several sophisticated methods to predict the likelihood of dying based on several criteria that measure the severity of an episode of pancreatitis. In all of those calculations, Mr. Evans had a less than 3% chance of survival. He was able to survive because of his strong mental attitude, his loving wife and her care, the excellent and complicated health care he received at several hospitals and from several physicians, and his strong faith in God.

Fortunately, Benji was cared for by some of the best pancreas experts in the country. Mr. Evans was fortunate in that he was cared for by several teams of doctors and nurses who are experts in the treatment of disorders of the pancreas and they did all the right things. Despite this, his ordeal was a nightmare for him and his family and his road to recovery was extremely long and bumpy. But, sometimes with the help of God, your wife, and good doctors, things turn out well. That is the case here, but for the grace of God.

i

***

A famous poet once said that "no man is an island." Benji Evans' *Back from Death's Doorstep* shows us why that is so.

Back from Death's Doorstep recounts Evans' two-year struggle against pancreatitis, a life-altering disease that suddenly struck him when he was just 35. It is a dramatic tale. The disease arrived unannounced and unexpected on Father's Day 2016, upending Evans' life and changing its course forever. Over the next two years, Evans would endure a medically induced coma, emergency medivac flights, and uncertainty over the disease's progression.

Despite his harrowing experiences, which he narrates with an eye for detail, Evans maintains a mischievous sense of humor throughout. Taking his 60 days in hospital and loss of nearly 40 pounds in stride, Evans joked about his new weight loss program (much to the distress of his wife). Later still, when complications from surgery resulted in a massive incisional hernia, Evans lovingly named it Brutus.

But Evans' two-year struggle makes clear that even his strong sense of humor has its limits. He openly describes his remorse over being cranky in the darkest days of his recovery and is frank about the emotional costs of being prescribed opioids during his treatment and recovery. In the end, *Back from Death's Doorstep* is not the telling of one person's struggle with a life-threatening illness, but rather how communities based on family and faith sustain and promote the well-being of us all.

—**Matthew Kelley J.D**. Attorney.

***

My heart hurt for Benji and his family as I read his story. I can't imagine the pain that everyone went through as they navigated uncertainty and the possibility of living life without the man that they love. However, this book encouraged my faith. I thought a lot about Hebrews 6:19, "We have this hope as an anchor for the soul, firm and secure." I was reminded that God is faithful. The presence of Jesus will steady us in terrible storms.

—**Leslee and Matt Holliday**, Hosts of *Table Forty podcast and retired Major League Baseball Player*.

***

This is a wonderful true story of someone who is truly loved by so many. His fascinating journey navigating a difficult and life-threatening illness is a saga of faith, love, and devotion. He is paying back this love many times over through his work with the Oklahoma Blood Institute. His story will warm your heart.

—**Ann McKennis**, RN, CNOR(E), CORLN(E) *The Woodlands, Texas.*

Back from Death's Doorstep

A story of faith and overcoming the odds

Benji Evans

Dedication

The list of people who helped my family throughout this ordeal would take 20 pages, even if I could list all of them. I hope each person who said a single prayer for me knows they had a significant part in my being here today. This book is a way for me to say thank you to each of you. You all kept me going, even during my bad days, with your words of encouragement that I received almost daily.

I specifically want to thank Dr. O'Neal for fighting on my side, even when it didn't look like there was a reason. You kept me alive when the odds were against me. To my nurse, Meg, who is now a special family member, I'm so glad you were there to keep me going and help my family. The doctors, nurses, physical therapists, pharmacists, people who cleaned the room, and every other person with whom I interacted at the hospitals, were all top-notch people in my book. The care I received throughout my stays in the hospital is just mind-blowing to me. You all kept me alive when the odds were against me. You are definitely special people and many of you alike to this day.

There are five people I met on September 29th, 2017 (and 37 I didn't meet) and it is very important for me to thank them. They literally gave a bit of themselves to keep me alive. David, James, Lisa, Monty, and Susan, I will never be able to thank you enough. "You gave, I lived!"

I have to thank my sister Jodi, her husband Jeff, my niece Reese, and my nephew Mason, for being huge prayer warriors and keeping all my friends and family updated on Facebook. Jodi's posts alone could make an entire book! She was there during the hardest days for my parents, Davina, and me. I pray that you know what that meant to us.

Glenn, Josy, Curtis, Becky, Liz, William, and Jerram, I am so blessed to have married into your family. Thank you for molding my wife into the person she is today.

My parents, Brad and Janelle, spent many nights living out of hotels and "apartments" during my many hospitals stays. I would hate to guess how many nights you spent in unfamiliar beds and eating nothing but restaurant food. Your faith was there when I needed it most, and you never gave up on me. I will never have words enough to thank you for raising me the way you did.

- To fight for what you want.

- Never give up.

- Life isn't easy.

- You can overcome!

I was blessed to have my wife Davina, with me; she was my rock throughout everything. Her faith never wavered throughout my, which helped me to keep my faith as solid. I will never be able to thank her enough for doing all the things she did. I don't think anyone expects to go through what we went through so early in our marriage, but it definitely made us stronger. Our third year of marriage wasn't one I want to repeat, but I look forward to many more years to come.

Love you. Mean it.

Published by KHARIS PUBLISHING, imprint of KHARIS MEDIA LLC.

Copyright © 2021 Benji Evans

ISBN -13: 978-1-946277-89-3
ISBN -10: 1-946277-89-4

Library of Congress Control Number: 2021931186

All KHARIS PUBLISHING products are available at special quantity discounts for bulk purchase for sales promotions, premiums, fund-raising, and educational needs. For details, contact:

Kharis Media LLC
Tel: 1-479-599-8657
support@kharispublishing.com
www.kharispublishing.com

TABLE OF CONTENTS

Acknowledgement

I would like to acknowledge the following people, without whose wonderful faith, help and assistance, this book would not have been possible. Thank you everyone.

Davina Evans – my wife
Brad Evans – my father
Janelle Evans – my mother
Jodi Evans Weyers – my sister
Dr. Dillon Roach, MD – a very good friend

Introduction

I'll never forget the night Benji was born. It was a Monday night and I was sitting in the delivery waiting room at the Ponca City hospital watching a Monday Night Football game. It was taking longer than it should take and I was getting concerned when I looked up and the doctor was getting on the elevator to go home. I ran out and asked him if everything was alright and his comment was "hasn't anybody talked to you"? My heart began to race as it sounded like there was a problem. All I had ever prayed for was to have a healthy child and hopefully a son. The doctor said come with me and I followed him to the nursery where he said "see that bed with the blue bow on it, that's your son"! I don't know that I've ever had a bigger smile on my face in my life! Now, I had someone to follow in my footsteps, to teach him about the great outdoors, work habits, and about our God that directs us in our daily lives. He was my miracle child and nothing but good times were in the future for us. I never would have thought thirty-five years later I would once again be praying for a healthy son.

Brad Evans – Benji's father

Chapter 1

Who I Was Then

This story is about the illness I went through in 2016-2017. I grew up in the small town of Blackwell, Oklahoma. From when I was a little boy, I enjoyed spending time outdoors, hunting or fishing with my dad, Brad. Hunting and fishing have been a passion of mine my entire life. My mom, Janelle, even went fishing with me while I was growing up.

My sister Jodi graduated high school five years before me. After I graduated from high school, I went to Northern Oklahoma College and then Oklahoma State University. After college, I worked as a lender for BancFirst™ in three small towns from January 2004 to July 2007. I had followed in my dad's footsteps, as he retired in 2018, after 42 years in banking. I then moved closer to home, to Ponca City, in 2007 and went to work for RCB Bank. The funny thing about that is, the president of the corporate offices of RCB also worked for the first bank where my dad first worked.

I was diagnosed as a Type 2 Diabetic in 2008. As a 28-year-old bachelor at the time, I had not done a good job of being active or eating healthy. Over the next eight years, things didn't change, and I didn't take care of my body like I should have.

In 2013, I married Davina, the love of my life. We had been married about two and a half years when our marriage went through the hardest thing you could ever expect to happen to two people, a life-threatening illness when I was 35.

In 2016 my life turned upside down...

The last picture of Benji before he got sick. He is on the far right

Chapter 2

The Glass Through Which I Look

Davina's Story

I came to Ponca City as a pharmacist at the hospital in 2006. Being a pharmacist was both a blessing and a curse, given what would happen 10 years later. Sometimes, you can know too much...

Benji and I started dating in May 2011. I jokingly tell people he picked the best year to introduce me to The St Louis Cardinals and baseball. That was the year they won the World Series. Benji played Little League baseball against Matt Holiday, who is from Stillwater, OK. He told me Matt could bat every third inning and pitch and win the game all by himself. He said it was never fun playing against him, so Benji was a Matt Holiday fan more than a Cardinals baseball fan. I thought baseball was boring when we started dating and I didn't realize they played almost every night during the summer. Oh, how things have changed!

I was blessed to have been born with an excellent memory. I somehow knew more about the current roster of the team than Benji did that year. It was really just by facial recall. By October, I would go home and finish watching the games there. Yadi Molina was my absolute favorite, thanks to Benji singing his praises.

I remember going home during Game 6 of the World Series that year. Benji had lost faith in his Cardinals at that point. Benji is a realist and very aware of the current situation; he knows the stats of winning or losing, especially in all-things sports. I knew the game wasn't over. I wanted to watch the end. The Cardinals came back and won in dramatic fashion.

Never base your future on your present or past. If you refuse to let your past go, it will kill you. Your present only defines your present, not your future. Yes, each of our pasts shape each one of us and affects our present and future, but it does not define us. Only God does that. God is the only One who knows our steps before we take them. His ways are higher than ours, and for that I am so very thankful. My ways are small. My world is small. But God's ways are always higher and all-powerful.

You see, I was raised in a home that built me to have a relationship with Jesus. They taught me about God from birth. I remember, as a young girl, praying that God would give me a godly husband. At the time, I didn't know what that really meant, I just somehow knew to pray for that man who would one day be my husband. Also, I was never the girl who imagined my wedding or had names picked out for my children. I didn't really want children. I didn't know other girls did pick out names until some girls at camp asked me what my kids' names would be when I had them! I made names up on the spot to fit in with all the other girls.

It's funny now but I didn't think much about it at the time. Now I know. God didn't design me with the burning desire to have children. He didn't design me to crave love so much that I felt like I needed a husband, or wanted a husband, or at least liked the idea of having a husband, but in fact, I really didn't need a husband.

"Perhaps this is the moment for which I was created."

Benji and I got married when I was 35 and he was 33. Neither of us had been married or had children from a previous marriage. That was a God thing. It was extremely difficult to find someone to date who didn't have children from a previous relationship. It was not easy finding another young professional in my community where it was "a great place to raise a family." That was what I was told in my interview at the hospital. And it *is* a great community, it just isn't necessarily easy to find a husband here. But GOD knew why I was here. I was here for Benji.

Benji and Davina May 2013

Benji and Davina September 2015.

The First Hard Thing to Happen

Heartache sits in all of us. In August 2015, my 75-year-old dad suffered a 90% occlusion stroke. It was a stroke from a clot in a location of his brain where surgery was not an option. One of dad's passions was mowing the lawn and pasture. He lived to have a well-manicured home. Apparently, he had decided to mow the yard when he had the stroke. He had been working outside with the hay haulers, in temps approaching 95 F.

Thankfully, he was in the front yard by the truck with the door open when Mom found him. She was inside the house and thought he was with the guys still working. They had probably left just before he came back to the house. We don't know how long he lay there in the heat before Mom found him.

I remember the phone call. It was on a Wednesday night. I don't remember the lesson at church that night. I do remember standing in the sanctuary that evening, toward the end of church. I remember Deuce, one of the assistant pastors, praying for me. He prayed for peace for me. He prayed for my home and marriage. I remember weeping that evening at church. I didn't know why; neither did he.

Benji and I grabbed an overnight bag and headed to the hospital. My parents lived almost three hours away and Dad's cardiologist was out of Oklahoma City. There was a bad thunderstorm that night. The helicopter pilot and crew could not fly from Okemah to OKC, so Dad was flown to St. John's in Tulsa. Later, I found out it had higher credentialing doctor was there than was available at the hospital in OKC, plus my friend Cody was a nurse practitioner at St John's.

What I do remember about that drive was once my initial distress wore off; the car was flooded with a sense of peace. Cody was on duty at the time; Dad was admitted to his unit.

BUT GOD!

Something just isn't right

June 18th, 2016 – Father's Day weekend 2016 we had planned on visiting my parents on the family ranch. Benji woke up Saturday morning before I did and made sausage gravy for himself. When I walked into the living room, he said he just didn't feel right. He said his stomach was kind of off. I thought that's odd, he didn't eat all of his breakfast. He had experienced the flu the week before. At least we thought it was the flu. We actually now believe it was his pancreas flaring up. His primary care physician had ordered topical Promethazine for nausea that week. It is his practice not to see patients with the flu. It's the right practice. I am a pharmacist. I know the guidelines.

Benji was a Type 2 diabetic. He was 35 but had been diagnosed a few years before we met. It really had never been controlled. His diet was not what it should have been. Sausage gravy was a rare treat for Benji. He really didn't eat it often. That morning it sounded so good to him or so he thought. I told him he didn't have to go to Okemah with me if he didn't feel well. He said he wanted to go so we started our fateful trip.

Benji

We left the house around noon to make the two-and-a-half-hour trip to my in-laws to celebrate Father's Day. Lunch was at our favorite Thai restaurant in Stillwater. After eating, I told Davina that I still didn't feel well, and felt if I could just throw up, my stomach would feel better. I'd thought I must be getting a bug, so it wouldn't be a good idea to be with her family. Her dad had a stroke back in September and his immune system was still down. The last thing I wanted to do was to give him whatever I was getting.

Davina wanted to take me home but I didn't want her to reach her parents any later than it already was. I said I could find someone to take me. I called Ryan and Jenelle who live in Stillwater to see if they could drive me back home to Ponca City. They were about to watch the Oklahoma State Cowboys play in the College World Series, but Ryan said to come over, hang out, and they would get me home later, but I knew I needed to get home where I could relax and would hopefully feel better.

I called another friend, Aaron, who said he could take me home in an hour if I could wait. I went over to Ryan and Jenelle's house to wait for him, while Davina went on to be with her parents. I got to Ryan's and Jenelle's around 2:00 pm, and Aaron showed up around 2:45. We then headed the 45 miles back to Ponca City. Jenelle would later tell me she knew that I was more than just sick at their house; she was really worried about me when I left.

Of course, when we got to my house Aaron wanted to watch the rest of the OSU game, but I just wanted to go to bed. We watched the game and Aaron headed back to Stillwater. I curled up on the couch, hoping for a couple hours napping, knowing I would feel much better when I woke up. After the nap, the cure-all of chicken and noodle soup was on my menu. Even that didn't make me feel any better.

I decided to head to bed around 8:30 pm, thinking a good night's sleep would make all the difference, but when I woke up around 11:00 pm, I decided something was really wrong! I drove myself to the emergency room at Alliance Ponca City Hospital. I remember when I was sitting with the triage nurse, she was asking me about my symptoms. There was only one problem with this. I really couldn't pinpoint any.

"Do you have a fever?"

99.3.

"Do you have any pain?"

Nope.

"Have you been throwing up?"

No.

"Why are you here?"

I responded, "Something just isn't right!"

This nurse must have thought I was crazy, but she took my temperature, blood pressure, heart rate, etc., and then moved me into a room in the ER. The doctor came in and I explained to him how I knew something was wrong, but I didn't have any symptoms I could identify. I am sure he thought I was completely crazy, as well, but he ordered tests and had the nurse draw blood.

At around 1:30 in the morning, I was still in the hospital and posted on Facebook, "Anyone in Ponca awake at 1:30 this morning?" I was looking for someone to bring me a cheeseburger or something to drink because I was tired of sitting around waiting for the doctor to tell me what was wrong. This is the last full memory I have until July 8th.

Chapter 3

Turn for The Worse

Davina

June 19th, 2016. Benji sent me a text this morning at about 7:30 and told me he had gone to the ER around midnight last night.

"Ok" I responded. "What did they say?"

"They think it is pancreatitis or gallstones. I am waiting to see the doctor."

"Oh, so they admitted you?!" I said. "I am on my way!"

Of course, I was slightly frustrated Benji hadn't called during the night. He didn't want me to drive three hours in the middle of the night. I packed my things and sent a quick text to our Pastor, Rick Hughes, asking for prayer. Rick asked what room Benji was in but I didn't know. I hadn't even asked him which room he was in when we talked on the phone. Pastor Hughes was able to visit Benji before church that morning. He told me what room he was in, he prayed with Benji, and said he would be back to check on him later.

At this point, I realized Benji could be in serious trouble. I remember hoping it was gallstones as I drove back to Ponca City. I knew pancreatitis for a diabetic could have very serious consequences. But then again, people have pancreatitis all the time and are fine. Benji is young and strong, I thought. He will be fine, I hoped. I was wrong.

I made it to the hospital in Ponca City around 11 am. By the time I get there, they had diagnosed Benji with pancreatitis. He was hot, thirsty, and in a lot of pain. He kept asking for ice chips or water, but couldn't have any. The standard treatment for pancreatitis is nothing by mouth. He was allowed only a limited amount of ice chips. It was extremely hard for me to see him so uncomfortable.

In typical Benji-fashion, after I had been there a while, he told me I might as well go home and rest, because there was nothing I could do there. I took him up on his offer. I worked at the hospital and knew the nurses. I trusted them and I knew he was in good hands.

I came back to the hospital around 5 in the afternoon. Benji was still just as miserable. I remember watching his monitor. His heart rate kept going up and his BP was slowly dropping. I didn't like it, but I still knew the nurses were keeping a close watch on it. Also, the nurses kept giving him insulin, but his blood glucose was climbing. It should have been headed the other direction. His nausea continued. The nurses tried to place an naso-gastric (NG) tube in to get rid of the bile, but Benji has such a sensitive gag-reflex that this failed. Finally, the nurse came in and asked if we preferred to go to Oklahoma City, Tulsa, or Wichita.

"You are transferring him?' I asked.

"Yes, he needs a procedure done called plasmapheresis, and we don't have the equipment to do it."

We had learned his pancreatitis had possibly been caused by high triglycerides. His triglycerides registered at >4500 (normal is less than 150), which was greater than the scale could measure! We decided OKC would be the best place to go. Later, we learned the decision very well could have saved his life.

Benji was transferred from a regular room to CCU. It wasn't until then that I started to get nervous. They asked me to sit in the family waiting room until they could get him settled. It seemed like it was a good 20–30-minute wait. I remember thinking, "I work here. It should be fine for me to go back with him." Yet I did as they asked and waited.

I took this time to call his parents and let them know they were flying him out. Janelle had lots of questions I really couldn't answer. I hadn't been told much yet, either. She wanted to know if they were flying him out instead of taking him by ambulance, due to how sick he was. At the time, I didn't have any answers for her.

After what seemed like a long wait, the CCU nurse came and got me. I had worked with Leatta, and she had done a lot of work in the ER. I knew Benji had a great nurse in her. I was strangely calm the entire time. She asked me how I was doing.

"Oh, I'm fine." And I really was.

I saw the medications they were giving Benji. They didn't have to tell me Benji was in diabetic ketoacidosis. I knew. Subconsciously, I knew he was not doing well, yet, I stayed calm.

Benji was still extremely lucid. When he learned he was going to be life-flighted out, he made me try to call his insurance company; he wanted to make sure the flight would be covered on his insurance. I didn't care, but of course Benji did!

Janelle

We hadn't planned anything for Father's Day, we were just going to fix a special dinner for the two of us and wait on the phone calls from both of the kids wishing Brad a happy Father's Day. Then, the CALL came from Davina. Benji was in the hospital, they were running tests to see what was going on, and she would keep us posted. I heard concern in her voice, but not panic, and I was so grateful she was with him. When Davina made the second call later in the evening that he was being life-flighted to Oklahoma City, I actually felt relief. They would know better about how to treat him than the hospital in Ponca City. In my mind, it might take a few days of IV antibiotics or such to fight whatever was going on, but oh, how little did I know.

We packed our bags and prepared to leave early in the morning for the hospital in Oklahoma City. We prayed and prayed and prayed for the doctors to know how to stop this illness. Neither of us slept. This would be the first of many nights we had our phones by our side while we tried to sleep. Countless times during the night, we would check them just in case we missed a call. To this day, on occasion, I will think I hear my phone ring in the middle of the night.

Jodi

June 19th started out like any other Father's Day. Church, lunch, and then an afternoon with the family. I received a group text from Davina saying Benji wasn't feeling well and had driven himself to the

ER in Ponca City late the night before. She was on her way there from Okemah, where she had been visiting her parents. Of course, when I got the news, I was worried, but didn't think too terribly much about it, because Benji hadn't been sick or anything. Davina said she would just send us updates once she got there. I remember her sending a text that they were running some tests but thought maybe he had pancreatitis. I had heard that word before but had absolutely *no* idea what it was or how much of an expert I was going to become on it in the next year. I also did not know to be very, very afraid of this horrible illness. I *definitely* did not know it could be fatal.

We went on with our evening as we waited to hear updates. Like I said, I wasn't too terribly concerned, because there was no reason to think anything too serious was going to come about. I suppose it's a good thing none of us knew what we were in for. We may not have been able to survive it if we had.

Later that evening, some of our very good friends, Brandon and Cindy Carrell, stopped by. Jeff and I were sitting on the back porch with them, visiting and having a glass of wine, when I got a phone call from my mom. She wasn't frantic, but I could tell by her voice something was very wrong. She told me they had sent Benji by life-flight and his condition had become very, very serious. They were taking him to Deaconess Hospital in OKC. My first thought was to immediately jump in my car and head north. However, because I had consumed two glasses of wine (which is so not typical of me), I decided I better wait until the morning.

I went to bed with a heavy heart. I didn't like knowing Benji was in a hospital and I wasn't there. That's my brother. My only brother! Things had just been "fine" with him, so we thought. I didn't understand how he could so suddenly be having this issue. I prayed to God for Him to save my brother before I was finally able to fall asleep.

Benji

Looking back at this time in the hospital, I remember one small thing from 1:30 Sunday morning until late Sunday night. Apparently, I was completely lucid and understood everything that was happening. For some reason, though, my mind doesn't want me to remember all I went through. I was lying in the bed waiting for the helicopter to take me to a larger hospital. I looked into the hallway and saw the paramedic for the helicopter. It was Blake Vowel, a guy I'd known my entire life.

Davina didn't know Blake, so she was mortified when I yelled out to him, "There is no way I am getting on a helicopter with his fat ass!"

He looked into the room and saw me lying in the bed, then he laughed, asked what was going on, and said he was glad to see me. They loaded me up on the helicopter and I told Davina good-bye, then off we went for the flight to Oklahoma City. I remember talking to Blake the whole trip and telling him how thirsty I was. He said he didn't have anything for me to drink. We landed at Baptist Hospital a short time later. They loaded me up in an ambulance and drove me over to Alliance Health Deaconess (Deaconess doesn't have a helipad). Blake grabbed a bottle of water from the

EMT in the ambulance and gave me just a lid full of water to quench my thirst. It was a life saver!

Davina

It took about two hours to drive from Ponca City to Deaconess Hospital. They had admitted Benji into the Critical Care Unit (CCU) when he got there. I walked into the unit but was asked to wait. I sat in the waiting room. I was the only one there. At the time, I didn't realize how unusual this was, but later, after spending many days there, the waiting room was rarely unoccupied.

After a short time, the physician came to speak with me. He introduced himself as Dr. O'Neal. He was about my age. I remember noticing that while he seemed young, his eyes held wisdom. Dr. O'Neal asked me what I knew.

"He has pancreatitis and is in diabetic ketoacidosis," I replied. Then I added, "Well, they didn't tell me that, but I'm assuming he is."

"Yes, Benji is in ketoacidosis," Dr. O'Neal said. "His kidneys are failing. His serum creatinine was 2 at Ponca City; it's 8 now. It's good he is here sooner rather than later."

Serum Creatinine (SCr) is a measure of kidney function. An adult with normal kidney function would have a SCr of 1. The quick rise in his SCr in such a short amount of time made me realize how sick Benji was.

"Oh, wow!" I responded.

"He is very ill," Dr O'Neal told me.

I nodded my head. He repeated it a bit slower this time. "He is **VERY** ill."

I nodded again. I asked about the visiting hours of CCU and if I could stay the night in his room. Dr O'Neal said while visiting hours were over, I was welcome to go see him, but it was the unit's policy not to allow overnight guests in the room.

Benji was happy to see me. His nurse's name was Rachel. She was sweet, capable, and very young. I stayed in his room for a while. Again, there wasn't much I could do. I asked Benji if there was anything, other than something to drink, I could get him. There wasn't. I gave my phone number to Rachel. I was going to get a bed in a hotel and would check in again with him in the morning. I asked if they could call me if they needed anything.

June 19th - The call came at 3 o'clock in the morning. I was sleeping so deeply that I didn't hear the phone ring. It had gone to voicemail. Rachel called and asked me to call her back. I did. She told me Benji was deteriorating and asked me to come back to the hospital.

I was only a few short blocks away. Finally, I was scared; my heart was racing. I remember praying on the way to the hospital that I would make it in time.

I walked into the CCU unit. Benji saw me before I saw him.

"Hi, Babe!" he called out from his room.

Benji has a loud boisterous voice. It echoed throughout the halls. His room was full of nurses and techs. Dr. O'Neal walked up to me from the nursing station.

"They are doing a sterile procedure right now. You can go in as soon as they have finished. But I'm afraid if he continues to trend the way he is going, he isn't going to make it," Dr O'Neal told me.

I took a deep, deep breath. Dr. O'Neal squeezed my shoulder. I will NEVER forget that moment.

"Does he have family?" he asked.

"Yes," I replied, "I will call his parents."

"I think that's a good idea." Dr O'Neal said. Then he continued to explain a little of what had happened. Benji's blood pressure was dropping and his heart rate was rising. He was in full kidney failure. Dr O'Neal told me the dopamine had infiltrated, but they had to get it in there. Something infiltrating was the last of my concerns. I just nodded again.

When I was able to go into his room, Benji seemed absolutely fine. I asked Rachel what had happened.

All she said was, "Well, he went away for a little bit." He had actually gone into cardiac arrest.

I asked Benji what he remembered about the last 45 minutes. "Nothing" he responded.

I called his parents and talked to his mom. I then called my sister Liz, who is a physician's assistant (PA) and lived 30 minutes away. I asked her to please come and wait with me. Even though it was outside of visiting hours, we were able to sit with Benji in his room until shift change, when all guests had to leave the unit. Liz talked me into going somewhere for breakfast. Food was the last thing I wanted. I pushed the food around on my plate. All I wanted was to be with Benji.

Janelle

Another CALL from Davina. I answered and she said it didn't look promising for Benji to make it. He had coded. He might die. We need to get there as soon as possible.

WHAT? HOW CAN THAT BE?

I've capitalized the word "CALL" because each one of these represented a time when we cried out to God for help, not just a prayer request for help, we actually cried out to God to save our son. I called Jodi to let her know she needed to get to OKC as soon as possible to see her brother. I didn't give Brad the details until we had almost reached the hospital; I just couldn't bear to speak the words, but he knew. We talked on the way, about how Deaconess was such a small hospital and we couldn't understand why he wasn't at Integris or OU Med Center.

Why on earth did they take him there?

Because it was GOD's Plan, that's why.

Jodi

At approximately 4:30 am, my phone rang. Absolutely scared me to death! It was Mom. Very calmly, she said, "Jodi, I need you to pack a bag and get in your car. It is not good." *Wait, what? Not good? Excuse me? What does this mean? Like, HOW not good?*

The second I hung up the phone with Mom, my precious husband took both my hands in his, and as we sat up on our knees in our bed, he prayed over me. He prayed for the Lord to save my brother, for a safe trip for me (I "might" be known for having a lead foot) and for us to trust Him in this situation. It was one of the most precious and treasured moments of our marriage.

I threw some clothes in a bag, grabbed some make-up and jumped in my car. It was still dark outside when I left. I could not stop shaking. My car could not drive fast enough. I wished I could've flown. I tried to be smart, because I am a wife and mom and did not want to crash my car because I was driving so fast.

But I needed to be there. For my brother! For Mom and Dad! For Davina! I had too much time to think. I didn't like it. So, I prayed. I'm not sure how many times I must have said the same simple prayer over and over: "Lord, please save my brother."

I usually loved time in the car alone; it is such a great time to reflect and solve all the world's problems. But this time was different. Mine was almost the only car on the road. It was just God and me. I talked to Him all the way there. One moment I will *never* in my lifetime forget was when a new song I had never heard before came on the radio. Little did I know, it would become my theme song for the next few weeks, and the year following. (It was "Just Be Held," by Casting Crowns. Definitely listen to this song.)

Those words hit me; I can still remember when the song came on, it was just as I was crossing the border into Oklahoma. My home! The sun was starting to come up, there were hay bales in the fields. I had tears streaming down my face and I was crying out loud. I *knew* God had sent me that song. Over the course of the next few weeks, I would hear it at the most opportune times. It was God speaking to me and reminding me of His presence. He is *always* with us.

Janelle

We made it...He is alive...We can talk to him...He knows we are there...For the two of us, this was all that mattered at this exact time. Dr. O'Neal was the CCU doctor when Benji arrived, and was still in the CCU when we got there. He didn't give us any encouraging info, but he also said he wouldn't give up trying to keep him alive. I will NEVER forget him saying this! What concerned me on this day was the doctor telling us we could spend as much time as we wanted with Benji. To me, this was *not* a good sign. It gripped my soul like a vise. There are rules for visitation in the CCU. The fact we didn't have to follow those rules was "all telling" to me. We were in a state of shock. There are no words.

Davina

When Liz and I made it back to the hospital, Benji's parents were there. His sister Jodi was not far behind them. Benji was still very uncomfortable, hot, and desperately wanted something to drink. I had one job: Very sparingly give him ice chips every 15 minutes. On this morning, his nurse's name was Jeff and he was a nurse I will never forget. They were trying to undergo plasmapheresis, a process that would filter out the triglycerides from Benji's blood. He coded when they had started this the night before, so they had decided to wait until morning before trying again.

One thing I will never forget is Benji's phone ringing. It was his good friend, Spencer. He didn't realize Benji had been flown out the night before. He was offering to bring him coffee.

Spencer: "Hey I am going to Starbucks. Want me to get you anything?"

Benji: "I am not in the Ponca hospital anymore. They flew me down to Deaconess last night."

Spencer: "WHAT?"

Benji: "Yeah it was bad. They almost lost me last night."

Spencer: "What are you talking about?"

Benji: "Yeah, I asked the doctor last night where I was on a scale of 0-10 with a 0 being the worst. He said I was a 3."

What? Benji had told me he didn't remember anything from the night before. I was finally able to get the phone away from Benji; as I grabbed it, I tried to process what Benji had said. Spencer wasn't just a good friend to Benji, he had become family to me as well.

I said, "Hello, this is Davina."

He asked if I was okay and this is when I finally broke down and cried. Before that moment, I had been calm. Nervous, very concerned, but I hadn't cried yet. Hearing Benji had been at a 3 on that scale from 0 to 10 during the night shook me to the core. In truth, I'm glad I overheard the conversation. I was due to have a good cry.

Jodi

Fast forward to my arrival at the hospital. I was not sure what to expect, but I can tell you what I found was *not* what I expected. Benji was on the Critical Care Unit (CCU) floor. I didn't even know it existed. Everything was sort of a blur for the next few hours, but what I do remember is meeting Benji's doctor, Dr. O'Neal.

He was about my age and very likeable. I think, outside of the circumstances, we would probably be friends. He was wonderful, but very solemn and matter-of-fact with the information he was giving us.

I was starting to realize the severity of the situation. Mom was right, it was not good. In fact, it was more than that, it was straight up bad. Almost hopeless from what the doctors were telling us.

But not for me, because I believe in a God who is bigger! A God who demands Faith the size of a mustard seed, and I had it. I was clinging to it. It was the one thing that would get me through the following weeks.

The first day, I also remember meeting a nurse named Jeff. He had the gift of calmness. When Jeff was in charge, I felt like everything was under control. Thank you, Lord, for giving him this gift. I believe he was an angel who works on earth, one of many with whom we came in contact at Deaconess.

Davina

June 20th: Benji was stabilized for most of the day, but he was having some trouble breathing, due to his abdomen significantly expanding. He looked like he

24

had triplets in his stomach, it was getting so big. The problem with this was that it was putting pressure against his diaphragm, which made it difficult for his lungs to expand and contract. With each contraction, they couldn't expand as much.

Dr. O'Neal asked the surgeon, Dr. Agee, if he would go in and see what was going on. Dr. Agee told him he didn't think Benji was stable enough to undergo surgery; he wasn't willing to do it at this time.

There really weren't many changes throughout Monday.

Davina

June 21st: I had left Ponca City so quickly on Sunday night that I hadn't brought my medication or made arrangements for our pets. Because Benji's family was there and he was stable, I drove home. The next morning, I was driving back to OKC when Janelle called. She asked me if I was almost there. I was still quite a bit away. She told me they had decided to intubate Benji to help his breathing.

What? That escalated quickly. We didn't talk long. I could tell she was scared. I was disappointed I didn't get to talk to Benji before they put him under.

A family friend was with his parents visiting Benji when they intubated him. She immediately called me back. Kim had worked as a surgical scrub tech, so she had a medical background. She was able to reassure Brad and Janelle, and answer all the questions they had. I was very thankful she was there that morning.

I made it to the hospital, but not in time to say hello to Benji before they intubated him. I had only been there a few minutes when a code was called for room 389 -- Benji's room. The charge nurse ran into the room to let us know it wasn't a true code. Benji had extubated himself!

Later, the nurse told us, "I turned my head for one second and all of a sudden he reared up and spit the tube out!" Despite agreeing to being intubated, Benji decided he didn't like the tube put down his throat. It took four people to hold him down to do it a second time.

Later in the evening, I saw Dr O'Neal in the hallway. He told me they had to completely sedate him, to intubate him. In his words, "He was a bull to get down!"

"Oh, I'm sure he was," I replied.

It was 18 days before the love of my life would speak to me again.

June 21st, Davina's Facebook post: For those of you who may not have heard, Benji Evans is in the hospital in OKC in critical condition with pancreatitis complicated by diabetes. Several of his vital signs are improving but he does have a difficult road ahead of him. We appreciate all of your continued prayers. God is FAITHFUL.

Janelle

Watching Benji trying to breathe was agonizing. There was nothing we could do to help him. He was also begging for ice chips during this time, but they made it very clear to all of us that too much could be deadly. Benji was *not* a happy camper when we wouldn't give him all he wanted.

We had always tried to make things better for our kids and there was nothing we could do to "fix" it. We were all trying to "hold it together" in the best way we could, both individually and together. I've often said we don't get a "practice run" on how we will react in times like this. My prayers weren't always only for Benji, they were about how we as a family would bless each other, love each other, be patient with each other, and hold each other up when we felt weak. My prayers were answered in ways I could not imagine.

When the decision was made to put him in a coma, to use a paralytic and restrain him, it almost was a relief; he wasn't struggling and wasn't in any pain. From the day he was put in a coma, it seemed to me like time stood still.

After Benji was in the coma, the first time I went into his CCU room I sat down in a chair on the right side of the bed and continued praying for a miracle; I laid out my heart to God. In my mind's eye, I vividly saw a vision of Jesus, standing right by my chair, with his right hand placed on his chest. I could feel Jesus in the room from that moment on. I KNEW He had a plan and He was in control, but in my heart, I hurt for Benji in ways I didn't realize were possible, until then.

To Benji: *They told us you they didn't know if you could hear us or feel us giving your hand a hug, so I decided maybe you could smell my perfume and know I was there with you. I'm sure they still talk about the crazy lady that put on so much perfume every day!*

By now we had finished making all the calls to family and friends we could make, using medical terms we didn't understand and sometimes couldn't pronounce, asking for their prayers. In the blink of an eye, prayers were being sent up by so many who loved Benji! We will forever be grateful for each and every prayer warrior!

We "set up shop" in the corner of the waiting room, because we didn't know what else to do. I slept in the waiting room more than a few nights, because I didn't know what else to do. I wrote down lab numbers, heart rate numbers, blood pressure numbers, any number I could find to give to Hank (a very close friend and retired surgeon from Texas), and Dillon, because I didn't know what else to do. The list would go on and on.

It seemed like they hung more IV fluids each hour and the CCU room was full of machines blinking and beeping. It was overwhelming to me. I prayed the doctors and nurses would never give up trying.

Dad found solace in watching and listening to Vince Gill and Carrie Underwood sing *How Great Thou Art*. He had it playing any time he had a few minutes to himself. He played it hundreds of times during these months, sometimes over and over. Each of us found something to hang onto, and collectively, we prayed.

Jodi

I hated seeing my brother in the condition he was in. He was very uncomfortable and irritable. He was having an extremely hard time breathing. The first few days, seeing him like that may have been the worst part of the entire experience. We all take the simple act of breathing for granted. Because he was so uncomfortable and having to work so hard just to breathe, which was causing additional problems, the doctor decided it would be best to go ahead and put him in a medically induced coma. WOW. I only thought they did that to people who were about to die. Little did we know…

Once Benji was put into the coma, he seemed a lot more at peace. I still did not like seeing him like this, but it was better than the alternative. He was so helpless, depending heavily on the machines to breathe for him, feed him, and keep him alive. The machines must have been working overtime.

I would come to his hospital room often, put my hand on his arm and just talk to him. I was good at giving pep talks. I was told he might not hear me, but I believed differently; I was his big sister and I had always bossed him around, so I wasn't about to stop now. I have never been so desperate for my brother to listen to me than I was at that time.

I needed him to follow my instructions: "Benji, I need for you to be tough. I need for you to work really hard and not give up. You can do this, Bubba. I know you can!"

So many prayers were said over him during this time. I was no longer begging the Lord to save him; I knew He would. Through this time, my prayer was about how we would give God all the glory for the miracle He was about to perform, and for us to be patient while all of us were in the process. I prayed about us being seen as a walking ministry to the nurses, doctors, custodians, and mostly to the family members of others in CCU with whom we would come in contact in the waiting room. Some of these people I now call brothers and sisters.

Dillon

I am an ER doctor. Benji and I have known each other about 18 years. Over this time, we have been great friends, roommates, fishing buddies, and we were groomsmen at each other's weddings. Just like I imagine most people reading this can probably remember where they were when they first heard about September 11th, I can remember exactly where I was when I found out Benji was sick.

My wife and I were vacationing in Grand Cayman. The last day of our trip, we were lounging on the beach when my wife saw a post on Facebook from Benji's wife, Davina, saying Benji was in the hospital diagnosed with pancreatitis. I immediately started texting with Davina and getting more details.

As I learned more and more about what was going on, the more and more concerned I felt. We were to fly home the next day, and I told my wife we needed to go see him. Thinking pancreatitis was something like appendicitis, she stated we had left our kids for a week and needed to relieve the grandparents, so she requested we wait a day to see him. I began to explain to her how sick Benji was, how serious his condition really was, to the point where I shared my concern he might die. I listed a few complications that could happen with pancreatitis and diabetic ketoacidosis.

Unfortunately, our flight was delayed and we got stuck for the night in the Houston airport. The next morning, we landed in Oklahoma City and drove straight to the hospital. This was the first time I was able to see him and hear, firsthand, how everything had been going. I'll never forget the first time I walked into his hospital room and saw one of my best friends laying in a hospital bed, on a ventilator, sedated, and paralyzed. Even though I knew how grave the situation was before coming, seeing it firsthand was truly staggering.

I'm an Emergency Medicine Physician. Seeing these situations is not new to me. I work at one of the highest acuity hospitals in the state; I see patients in dire situations almost every shift. It was completely different seeing one of my best friends in such a situation.

Unfortunately, at that point, when I was explaining to Laura, my wife, all the complications Benji could have happen from this severe case of pancreatitis and diabetic ketoacidosis, I didn't know he would have every complication imaginable. Over the next few weeks, I would come by to see Benji after work or on my off-days. While sitting in the CCU waiting room, I talked with Davina, Benji's parents, his sister, and other friends and family. It was extremely surreal and heart-wrenching. Part of me wanted to be encouraging and positive to his family and friends, but at the same time, from a medical standpoint, I knew all the ways this could still go terribly wrong. I tried to keep a balance between being positive for a family that needed hope and encouragement, but also trying to prepare them that Benji may never recover and he still may not make it through this. We talked about what his doctors had said each day, we'd break down what was going on currently, and what each next step in his possible recovery would be.

Davina

June 22nd: Dr O'Neal and the surgeon, Dr Agee, agreed Benji was stable enough to have surgery. Before that, they had said he wasn't stable enough to leave the room! The goal of surgery was to relieve pressure in his abdomen (he had what is called abdominal compartment syndrome which is an abnormally increased pressure within the abdomen). Benji was in kidney failure and was struggling to breathe due to the high volume of fluid his pancreas was releasing.

Dr. Agee made a 14-inch incision in his abdomen and removed fluid. They told us there was too much fluid to fully see the pancreas. What they could see of the pancreas was black, which meant it was necrotic or dead tissue. Because Benji's pancreas was still actively dying, they elected to not sew the incision site closed. They packed it and covered it with bandages. Benji was then placed on paralytics so he would not accidently jostle the wound. At that point, Benji was both sedated and medically paralyzed. Life was very grim.

Janelle

Days were a blur now; one day ended and another began. Some days were just exhausting, because it seemed like they weren't *doing* anything to help Benji. Other days, it seemed like they were hurrying too much. Both of those thoughts would be swirling in my mind at the same time; like I said, it was exhausting. Then the day came when Dr. Agee said he felt Benji was stable enough to do surgery. I had no idea what this meant, but the nurses said he wouldn't be trying the procedure if he didn't think Benji was stable enough to get through the surgery. I took it as the best news ever. They weren't just keeping him on the machines to keep him alive, they were actually doing *something* to help him get better. Seeing him on the gurney and leaving for surgery was gut wrenching. We fervently prayed we would be able to see him again.

Jodi

A few days in, and Benji had to go into surgery. I honestly don't even remember the details as to why now, but I do remember it was going to be very risky. I had never seen Mom and Dad so helpless. I knew (like the song said) I needed to step up and be strong for them. It was a role I was ready to fill. They wheeled Benji past the waiting room and down the hall for surgery; that is another visual memory that will stay with me forever. It was a *huge* relief when we got word he had made it through. His wound would remain open for a good week or so before they would close it back up. I had a hard time wrapping my brain around this, but they knew what they were doing. Lord, thank You for giving men the ability to perform life-saving surgeries and having the confidence to do so! They must also be angels on this earth. Now it was time to pray against infection.

Jodi's Facebook post: Our family would appreciate your prayers for my brother. We feel your love and concern and can't thank you enough for all the offers to help. If you know Benji, you can imagine how hard this is for him...he is a fighter and we are fervently praying him through this!

Jodi Evans Weyers is with **Davina Evans** and **Janelle Uhrig Evans**.

June 22, 2016 · 🕸

A lot of you have been asking for updates on **Benji**. Without sharing too many details (if you know him, you know he would not like that), wanted to let everyone know he is going to be in CCU at Deaconess in OKC for awhile. His doctor said to not expect any less than 2-3 weeks. The good thing is that they have put him in a medically induced coma, so he is able to rest.

If you would like to visit, that would be just fine. My parents and Benji's wife, Davina are on the 3rd floor camping out in the waiting room (no need to check in, just come on up). They had lots of visitors yesterday and it was such a blessing and encouragement to them. Distractions from the constant worry have been a good thing. They are so blessed by wonderful friends!

Thank you all for your constant prayers and concern. Our family feels your love! 💜 💜 💜

👍❤️ 209   84 Comments   17 Shares

👍 Like   💬 Comment   ↪ Share

June 22ⁿᵈ – Jodi's Facebook post

Davina

June 23ʳᵈ Davina's Facebook post: We have a bit of good news. Benji's kidneys are functioning now; this made the doctor say that "we may be starting to beat it." He remains on a ventilator so that he will not move and disrupt the incision on his abdomen. He will likely remain on the ventilator through Tuesday

After I posted on Facebook, I thought things could not get worse. They did.

We were told Benji had developed blood clots. He was on a heparin drip to prevent this, but he still developed several clots. We knew there was one in his arm. Our big concern was that one would develop in his lungs or brain and cause irreversible damage. Also, Benji's white blood count was plummeting and dangerously low.

The hematologist was consulted. Dillon and I were in Benji's room when he reviewed his chart. He determined that Benji's white count began falling soon after the first-time heparin was given. My husband was allergic to heparin!

I distinctly remember my stomach dropped briefly; it was slight. I knew heparin was the standard for care. I also knew very few people were allergic to heparin. I simply dismissed my misgivings because I had no basis for them. I assumed it was because I knew heparin required close monitoring and required frequent dosing adjustment. While working at the hospital pharmacy in Ponca City, I helped develop and write heparin orders and monitoring guides. Less than 5%, closer to 1%, of all patients taking heparin develop heparin-induced thrombocytopenia (called a HIT). This is a condition in which low platelets develop, due to blood clots. But, of course, Benji was in that 1%!

This was the day when I was most scared. I knew Benji was very sick, but it wasn't until this day that I thought I could be losing my husband. Brad and Hank were pressing Benji's nurse, Nicole, about his condition. She was about my height, a petite, dark-headed nurse. Brad and Hank were both tall men. Neither was being ugly or belligerent, but I wanted to diffuse the tension. But Nicole said, "I will tell you this, I have seen worse recover." I realized then that there was no calming the guys and I retreated to the waiting room.

The worst day of this was also the evening my strongest support showed up. Our pastor and his wife had visited several times. The rest of the ministry team and dear friends had been praying earnestly, but without being aware of the extent of Benji's condition, they all showed up that evening. Chuck Allen told me he "felt pressed to come." The Holloways and their boys also popped into the waiting room while the Allen's were there. Bill Monden, another minister and friend, came as well.

I took Bill back to Benji's room. He stood across the bed from me. I had tears streaming down my face. Bill told me "to trust the God that brought us together, to keep us together." Once again, I could only nod my head. Words would not come. But there could not have been more timely or comforting words. I *still* cling to those words.

God could not have given me a clearer message. He sent the people I needed, the ones whose faith and prayers would lift me, on the day Benji was the most critical. It was simply one more affirmation God was in control and I could trust Him. *God is faithful!*

During the times Benji was in the hospital, I decided to send him emails. It was a way for me to say the things I needed to say to him. Even though he wouldn't be able to see them for quite some time, it was an outlet for me.

My email to Benji: I'm missing you so much. I'm so thankful you are in my life. You are my greatest blessing. I'm ready for you to come back now. Love you...mean it. So, so much....

Jodi

There is one particular thing that happened to put me in a panic. Benji developed a visible blood clot in his arm. It was very serious and had the potential to end everything. My prayers, life and faith were strong. I marched into his room by myself on that day, laid my hands on his arm in the exact spot of the blood clot, and prayed that sucker away.

No, really! I did! I knew it at that very moment. I'm not sure that I have ever been so confident of anything in my whole life. I walked out of the room with 100% confidence the blood clot was gone, not because I'm magic, but because He is good!

I believed by faith the Lord had removed it. As I prayed, I promised God I would give Him the glory for what He had done. I have still not stopped telling people about that one!

The first day or so, we spent a lot of time going back and forth from Benji's room to the nurse's station, to the waiting room. Terms we had never heard before were being thrown at us left and right. I learned triglycerides are a thing you don't want to be too high; for Benji, they had skyrocketed. I now have mine checked at least once a year. I learned there is a machine called a "plasmapheresis machine," which removed his triglycerides by filtering out the "bad blood" and replacing it with "clean blood." Whoever invented this machine must be a pure genius! I also learned not every hospital was equipped with one, but Deaconess was. Thank you, Lord, for this gift! Again, it was no coincidence where Benji ended up.

I learned how to read hospital monitors: Heart rates; blood pressure, and not just how to read them, but how to obsess over them. Those numbers were what we were holding onto every day. They were scary numbers. I didn't always like them. The nurses and doctors didn't like them either. I studied every detail of their facial expressions in order to get a feeling of what emotions they were carrying. I wanted to catch a glimmer of hope in their eyes. All I could see was fear.

On day two or three, Nurse Jeff went home and Benji got a new nurse. Her name was Meg. The first time I saw her I thought, "Well, isn't she a cute little thing?" Once I got to spend some time with her and watch her work, I realized not only that she was a cute little thing, but also, she was feisty, efficient, intelligent, God-loving, and a crazy-good nurse. She had worship music playing in the hospital room, and guess what song came on? *Just Be Held.* (Thanks Lord, another reminder You are still here.)

I got comfortable enough with Meg that I was able to ask her if she thought Benji was going to make it. I had faith he would, but hearing it from an expert was going to be good for my mind. Her answer didn't make me feel better. She reiterated just how critical Benji's condition was, and said it would basically take a miracle for him to come out of it.

Okay. I'll take it. She didn't say no. I know my brother and I know my God; the odds were good, at least in *my* mind.

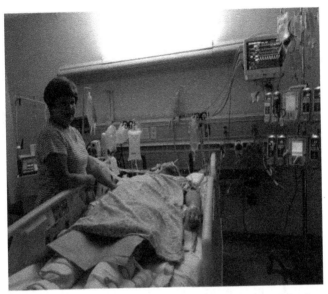

Janelle standing over Benji while he is in a coma and intubated on June 23rd, 2016.

Davina

Another dreaded call came during the night. The nurse had elevated Benji's bed and his blood pressure crashed. Oddly enough, I don't remember the nurse's name. All I heard was his BP had dropped to 20/10. The nurse told me he gave Benji 15 compressions and it returned to normal; he also told me they had decided to not raise his bed again!

I was sharing a hotel room with Benji's parents and his sister Jodi. I was on autopilot. I told them what happened, and that the nurse said his vitals were fine and he wasn't in distress. Benji's parents, of course, were going to the hospital, no matter what I did or said.

Jodi and I decided to stay in the hotel room; we were exhausted. So were his parents. We asked them to call us if they thought we should come in. Thankfully, all was well, or as well as things were in Benji's world.

Thankfully, this was the third and final time Benji coded. The surgery team debrided Benji's incision site three more times over the next week. The days became blurry and seemed like they were all the same that week. Benji's condition was still very critical. He didn't improve, but he wasn't declining, either. I pushed through, again on autopilot.

Janelle

Davina answered the CALL during the night that Benji had a code blue episode. Brad and I went to the hospital so we could relay the info back to Davina and Jodi, who stayed at the hotel. This new nurse had big eyes, and some of the regular nurses who were on the code just gave a slight shrug, so I couldn't read what their expressions meant. All I knew was, he didn't have the nurses we had learned to love around him. I didn't leave until the next shift change. It was the <u>only</u> time I just didn't feel at ease with the staff.

We had grown to love all the staff who helped Benji, from the respiratory therapists to the nurses, to the housekeepers. They truly cared, and we loved them for that.

Every few days, we would go to the surgery waiting room while Dr. Agee would unpack Benji's abdominal incision for more debriding. Each of those days, when he walked out of surgery with a grin on his face, meant that was a *good* day. We learned to appreciate his honesty and his rare bit of humor, but most of all, his courage to do the surgery on a very sick young man.

Jodi

Another moment that stands out is when nurses Jeff and Meg had gone home for the day, and Benji had not had a good day. I'm guessing this was maybe five to six days in. He got a new nurse that evening, who was a traveling nurse. I did not get a good feeling from him. I am sure he was a perfectly good person and capable nurse, but I knew he didn't know us. He didn't know Benji and our family, not like Jeff and Meg did. I didn't feel he would put up a fight for Benji, which probably wasn't the least bit true.

That night, as Mom, Dad, Davina and I got settled into bed at the hotel, we got the phone call no one could ever imagine receiving. Benji had code-blued. Wait a minute, that's real? I thought this only happened on *Grey's Anatomy*, *not* to my brother! Mom and Dad rushed to the hospital; Davina and I prayed. And processed. And prayed some more. I waited on pins and needles to get word from Mom and Dad. Finally, we heard Benji was okay. *Thank you, Jesus. And please no more code blues.*

Davina

June 24th Davina's email to Benji: I decided to drive home tonight. Your head moved today. I hope you aren't in any pain/discomfort. I don't know how to express how I feel. I love you. I miss you. Can't wait for you to be home with me. You are the best thing that has ever happened to me. You balance me out. You are the calm in my storm. You love me when I'm unlovable. Just come home to me. Love you so much.

Jodi

I was able to go home for a couple days over the weekend after the first week Benji was in the hospital. I loved and gave love to my family, but really just wanted to be back at the hospital. I got some family and pet therapy during that time, then went back after two days. The first week I was there, I missed my son Mason's 10th birthday. It really hurt this Momma's heart. From my post in the windowsill in the wing being remodeled, I was able to throw together a small birthday party for him after his baseball practice. My sweet friend, Cindy, and her two girls brought balloons and decorations for the back room at The Pizza Place. I ordered a cake from HEB™. Someone sent me a video of the team singing "Happy Birthday" to my boy. I cried. Sometimes, things are just not meant to be missed. It was the one time I was absolutely torn up.

Dillon

A few days after Benji was admitted, I was sitting in the ICU waiting room with my parents. I saw one of the surgeons who worked both at my hospital and at Deaconess, where Benji was; she was walking back to the CCU. The surgeon friend asked what I was doing there and I told her who I was there to see. The look of shock and concern on her face was unnerving. On this day, she was covering for the surgeon who had done the surgery to relieve his abdominal compartment syndrome; she had seen Benji a few times and understood how bad his outcome would probably be.

Janelle

There are *so* many physicians who are trying to help Benji recover. We would go to the hospital very early each morning, in case any of the doctors had an update. They knew where we were. Coffee in hand, we were sitting in the corner of the CCU waiting room, waiting for any info we could give Hank and Dillon so they could "translate" for us. Even with "translation," we didn't have a clue what was going on! Almost all the doctors showed compassion, but I have to say there were a couple who needed to have a refresher course in that area. I remember that once Dr. O'Neal had said not to listen too much to the other doctors, as he would be the one who would say when Benji had "turned the corner." By the way, the most he ever said about that was, "We're about to reach the corner I was telling you about."

To be honest, most mornings we didn't need any doctors to say how things were going. When we walked in the doors of CCU, it was very evident on the nurses' faces if it had been a good night or a bad night; if the numbers were too high or too low; and if they felt confident or not. I hope we were able to express to them how much we appreciated them, how many times we prayed for them, and how we *know* God used them to save another life.

Grateful and Thankful!

Davina

June 27ᵗʰ – Davina's email to Benji: I drove home again tonight. Today was a much better day. They sewed up your incision. Your kidneys are not doing as much as I would like, but things are trending in the right direction. I just want to say I love you more than I know how to express. Come home soon.

Jodi

Jodi's Facebook post: Update on my brother this morning: After a couple days of not so encouraging news, we started our day with some fantastic news today! Benji's surgeon was able to sew his abdominal incision up completely, which was a HUGE deal and big time answered prayer. His doctor told us this morning he thinks we will be trending upward now as far as his recovery goes, as opposed to downward. Praise! Specific prayers today include seeing more self-sufficiency as far as the ventilator goes, increased kidney function (doing sooooo much better already!), and no blood clotting so he can receive dialysis. We are praising God for all He is doing and for the comfort and peace He is giving us. Thank you all for your continued prayers. Benji is so loved!

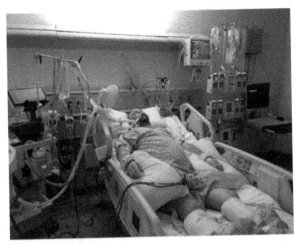

Benji hooked up to multiple machines keeping him alive on June 28th, 2016.

June 28th – Jodi's Facebook post: Prayer warriors, we have a specific request for you this afternoon. Benji is dealing with some pretty serious blood clotting issues. Please pray for this to be resolved, as it can cause other complications. We have so much faith that God is healing Benji; this is just a small setback

Jodi Evans Weyers is with **Davina Evans** and **2** ••• **others**.

Jun 29, 2016 · 👥

This is a picture of my brother's happy place - a little piece of heaven on earth which our family refers to as "The Cabin". So many priceless memories have been made here...so thankful. Continue to pray for his complete healing. He is receiving platelets this morning, so specific prayer that his body accepts those is appreciated. 🙏❤️🙏

👍❤️ 355   81 Comments   38 Shares

June 29ᵗʰ – Jodi Facebook post

June 30ᵗʰ – Jodi's Facebook post – Update on Benji this morning and specific prayer requests:

- Platelets. They are up from yesterday, but still need to see an increase.

- Going to start backing off a little on sedation today, which should help blood pressure stabilize, and allow us to communicate with him a little more.

- Pray for kidney function to continue to improve.

Thank y'all for covering him and our family in prayer. Your prayers, love and support are carrying us.

Also, if you know an ICU nurse, please hug their neck today. They. Are. Angels.

Davina

July 1st, Davina's email to Benji: You're doing better. It made me so happy to see recognition when you looked at me this morning. I'm so sorry you are going through this. Miss you lots. Looking forward to having many happy years together. Love you, mean it.

Jodi

Jodi's Facebook post - Update on Benji this morning:

- They have decreased sedation even more this morning. Our sweet nurse, Meg, has asked for no stimulation as he begins to wake up, although we can stand at his doorway and pray. The "waking up" process can take a day or two.

- Platelets are still too low. Keep praying those up.

- He will be pretty uncomfortable as he wakes up. So, prayers for him in that area. Not a real fun process, but we'll take it, as it means he is still on the road to recovery.

The grandkids are coming to visit Mimi & Grandad & Aunt Davina this afternoon. It is going to be a good day.

Family, Friends Old and New – in the Waiting Room

Jodi

Let me just say, at this point, I am beyond thankful for the amazing husband I have. With it being the month of June, he was able to stay home and take care of the kiddos while I stayed the week in OKC. I never once felt guilty about it, and knew he had it under control. Additionally, if he didn't have it under control, I had a village of girlfriends calling, offering their help, and ready to step in and take over at any moment. #Villeage. We are so blessed!! The texts and phone calls I was getting during this time was motivation for me to stay strong. It was incredible how many people were praying for my brother. Posting updates on Facebook daily was one way I was able to stay sane. I'm not sure how much Benji appreciated it, but it was one of the ways I was able to cope. Get it all out there. Have people bathe my specific requests in prayer. Blood pressure is too low - need prayers. Heart rate too low - need prayers. Triglycerides too high - need prayers. Oh my goodness, a blood clot has appeared - NEED PRAYERS!!!! Knowing how many people were praying for Benji helped increase my faith and hope. Prayer works. I had a windowsill I would sit in at the very end of the hallway. It was down the wing in a part of the hospital that was being remodeled so there was no one down there. It was my post.... My peaceful spot... My happy place.... Where I could regroup and recharge. Let the sunshine in.

Janelle

"THE MINISTRY OF PRESENCE" - I had no idea what this meant...but I learned quickly the true meaning of service to others in this ministry. Family and friends came in droves...and I mean droves! So hard to know where to begin: The Evans' Family arrived quickly! It was truly a time when both of us felt so very thankful for each and every one of them! I also remember when Benji had the blood clot appear. The first-person Brad called was his brother Bryan, and asked him to get to OKC as soon as possible. Brad literally fell into his arms when Bryan arrived. So thankful they could be at the hospital at that time; it lifted Brad up when he felt so low.

Brad's youngest brother, Jeff, sister, Dalanna, and her husband, Rod, made many trips to OKC. One thing I remember clearly is the first time they saw Benji in the CCU. It was certainly a scary thing for them to see, as he was already in the coma. As the weeks went on, and more and more and more machines and IV's were needed, their next time to walk into CCU was even more of a shock to them. The looks on their faces said it all. I was sad for them, because it was no longer a shock to me but it was a part of everyday life.

Brad's cousin, Steve, and his wife, Cherrie, made multiple trips to OKC. Those memories are precious to us, now more than ever. One *very* early morning, Steve walked into the waiting room and Brad said, "What are you doing here so early?" Steve said he was just on his way home to Kansas from South Texas, and thought he would stop by. Brad mentioned Oklahoma City wasn't on the way home from South Texas to Kansas. Steve just kind of shrugged his shoulders and said he never was very good with directions. He had driven all night from South Texas to OKC, just to be with us and check on Benji.

Then there are cousins Gary and Loretta, who were with us in the bad times and lifted us up with their humor and presence. Later, they were with us to celebrate the good times by attending the OBI night and then again for the one-year celebration!

Our "Okie Families and Friends" started to arrive almost immediately. There isn't any possible way I could ever designate if these people are friends or family; they are special to us beyond words, and there isn't a known "box" to put them in. So, we are *very grateful* for each and every one of them, for their prayers, and when they picked us up and supported us, when we felt we could not stand anymore. Of course, the Saralyn Drive (the street Benji grew up on) families visited: the Taylors, the Purdy's, the Bella's, and Marolyn all visited multiple times. After all, Benji was and is a part of each and every one of their families, just as they are to us. When one of us hurts, we all hurt. When one of us celebrates, we all celebrate.

D.W. and Jackie were the friends who prayed for us, cried with us, laughed with us; sometimes they just sat with us for hours and hours in the CCU waiting room or the surgery waiting room. There are not enough words to thank them for all they did for our family!

Then there were our friends, Jon and Barbara. I remember so vividly Barbara arriving. She looked at me and said, "Well, where is he...I've got some praying to do." I don't think *anyone* could have stopped her from going into his room to make the request for healing and miracles! She actually had a bottle of holy water that she put on the doorway, to bless everyone that came in. She is a prayer warrior everyone wants on their side!

Roy and Ruby were so very helpful to us in so many ways. They picked up clothes to launder, and checked on us daily to see if we needed company or being alone time. They had been through a family tragedy and they prayed for and with us every step of the way. Bill and Linda Rodgers brought food, offered their home to us, and visited so often. We had no idea they would be a vital step in God's Plan for healing Benji.

Hank, Nita, and Sue came up from Cleburne, TX numerous times. I remember Nita standing in our closet in Cleburne on facetime so I could tell her what clothes to bring to us...that's a true friend! Hank and Nita were our lifelines to the medical terminology the doctors were using and tried to explain all those lab numbers I gathered every morning. Looking back, it must have been a very trying time for them. We didn't, and still don't, have a clue what all those medical terms meant.

Jodi gave me a notebook and I was supposed to write down everyone who visited, but I failed miserably at that job. I wish now I would have asked everyone to sign the book. I'm sure the signatures would run into the hundreds in just the first week.

Davina's family, friends, and church family arrived to lift her up.

Jodi's friends arrived to lift her up.

Our friends arrived to lift us up.

And then Benji's friends arrived. Oh my, so MANY of them! Blackwell friends, NOC friends, OSU friends, bank friends, Ponca City friends, hunting friends, the list goes on.

Some of the friends were very animated and didn't mince any words in talking to Benji while he was in the coma... Saying he needed to be strong and he needed to get well and he needed to pay attention to what they were saying. Some were silent and never spoke a word while visiting him. Some prayed over him with a fervor I had never seen before. Some kissed him with tears streaming down their faces. One carried the burden of knowing too much medical information, but at the same time, never giving up the faith. Some saw him once and didn't choose to see him again in the coma but visited us in the waiting room often. They, like the rest of us, were all dealing with it the best we could.

Chapter 4

The Ministry of Presence

For these friends, for this family, we are so very grateful and thankful!

Jodi

As we spent most of our time hanging out in the waiting room, we were super-blessed by visits from friends and family. If you ever wonder if it's worth your time to visit someone who is in the hospital or has a loved one in the hospital, IT ABSOLUTELY IS! Those visits sustained us, kept us going. People brought snacks, took us to lunch, brought lunch, flowers, cards...it was love wrapped up in the act of service.

I knew Benji was loved, but holy cow! The number of friends from his childhood, along with new friends he made over the years, was overwhelming. Seeing grown men cry, specifically Drew and Fed, brought me to my knees. Getting teary-eyed again as I think about it now. These are dudes who were little terrors in their youth, along with my brother. They are now husbands, dads, business owners, hard working men... men, who all love my brother.... They will probably never know how much their visits meant to us. The way they prayed over Benji in his hospital room and cried like babies. Those were his people. They were, and are, *our* people. They are the good ones. If only everyone could be so blessed; it's one of the benefits of living in a small town, really. Taking those friendships with you for life...FOR LIFE!

Not only did my brother's friends come to visit, but also longtime friends of my parents. It meant the world to them to have them there, and it always refueled their tank. Laughter is good medicine, and with D.W. and Jackie Boyd around, there was always sure to be plenty of that. Having Jon and Barbara there was a blessing, as well. Barbara is the best prayer warrior I know. She is an angel on earth.

Roy and Ruby Wile were a complete Godsend. They would bring food and take our laundry home with them. And sometimes they would just sit and visit, let my parents talk. They had been through a tragedy of their own, and they knew how to minister to people in the midst of moments like this. It was such a blessing. Just people loving people...

And who could forget the visits from the Taylors and Purdy's. They will *always* be family. Having Heath Thompson (a friend of mine from high school) there several times was so good for my soul. Heath has been through a medical trauma and understands the recovery process is a marathon, not a sprint. What an encouragement he was to me. We talked about who we were then and who we are now. My, how the Lord has worked in our lives.

The Gillespie's; Catina, Brian Howard; John Koehler; Brandon Kahle; Tyke and Mandy; Spencer and his family; Kyle Reser; Chad Bechtel...gosh, too many to name and I know I'm forgetting a bunch. All had a huge part in carrying us through the darkest moments of our lives so far. You were a light and God was using you. Thank you.

Having our family members come to visit was the best. Even Mom's cousin, Jan Roop, came. I hadn't seen her in years and years, but I felt like she was a dear friend. She has a laugh that is contagious and reminded me of her mom, my mom's aunt.

The Browning's, Uncle Jeff, Uncle Bub and Aunt Sarah, thank you. Having you there felt like home. The visit from Steve and Cherie became a cherished one, as we lost Steve to cancer the next year. Thank you for being there and for the memory. The picture we got of Dad and Steve is now a precious treasure.

Steve and Brad during a visit to the ICU.

One of the guys we met in the waiting room was named Cody, and Cody was just a good ole boy. You could tell he hadn't had an easy life. His mom was in CCU. He couldn't afford to stay in a hotel at night, so he would push a couple couches together and sleep there. Mom brought him pillows from our hotel. Cody was now family. His mom was very touch-and-go. It didn't end well for her. Cody eventually left the hospital without his momma. My heart was sad. Lord, give him peace and guide him through life.

Every morning when we came to the waiting room, we would exchange medical updates with all our new friends. Many were like us, hanging on to every shred of information from the doctors that was in the least bit positive. I can remember Dr. O'Neal using the phrase, "He's not out of the woods yet," a lot. I did not love it, but I remember thinking, "But he's not gone yet, either." *You've got this, Benji.*

Dillon

I remember getting phone calls and texts from Benji's parents and Davina about all the different twists and turns, especially over those first 18 days in the coma. I remember the sinking feeling when I first heard about him coding, and how his physicians were concerned that even if he lived, it was possible his brain would never be the same. The first 10-14 days he just seemed like he wasn't getting any better. It felt like he would make just a little progress and then would take a big step back. Those first few weeks of Benji being in the hospital were so surreal. His parents and Davina had set up camp at a table in the corner of the CCU waiting room. The three of them, as well as his sister, spent hours and hours there each day. He didn't know they were there. He was sedated and, on a ventilator, but they were there each day, keeping up the vigil. The number of people I got to meet sitting in the corner was truly staggering. Extended family, family friends, childhood friends, and current friends I had never met. Benji was and is truly loved by so many, and has touched so many lives.

Jodi

Another positive thing that came out of my brother's illness was how close I was able to become to my sister-in-law, Davina. With them living in Oklahoma, I hadn't been able to spend much time with her before this. She was such a trooper throughout this whole thing. I know, when she married Benji, she was never expecting to go through something like this. I watched as the Lord molded and refined her faith. She amazed me. Looking back on it, I almost feel bad because she knew too much, she understood most of what was happening because of her medical background as a pharmacist. Mom, Dad, and I were probably better off, because ignorance is (can be) bliss.

Bless Davina's heart. She would go on to be a full-time wife, nurse, caregiver, pharmacist, helpmate, angel on earth for the next year. Words will never express how grateful we are for her! Those are some big shoes only she could fill. She has too many jewels in her crown to begin to count. She is the true result of many years of answered prayer. God bless her!

Dillon

We kept wondering when he would have to get a tracheotomy, because he couldn't get off the ventilator. They kept putting it off, and I worried about the long-term complications from being on a ventilator for so long. I have this very vivid memory of one of the last days he was on the ventilator. At this point, they had turned off almost all of the sedation he was on to keep him comfortable while intubated. He still had not responded to anyone, so there was still a huge question hanging over everyone, about how much brain function he was going to have.

I was back in his room with Brad, Benji's dad. We were talking and Benji opened his eyes and looked at us. He was very sleepy and somewhat sedated still, but was able to acknowledge we were there and shake his head a couple of times. It was so encouraging and felt like such a big blessing. They were finally able to remove the breathing tube the next day, and it was such a huge step in the right direction.

Davina

July 3ʳᵈ – Davina's email to Benji: I hate that you're not here with me. I told you I missed you and you gave me a thumbs up sign. We're going to make it. I love you so very much.

Jodi

Jodi's Facebook post – Benji update:

There hadn't been a whole lot of changes until this morning - Dr came in and for the first time said EVERYTHING is trending upward!!!! Woo hoo!!!! Still need platelets to come up and she's continuing to give him blood transfusions to help the pancreas heal. He is STABLE!!!! Praise the Lord!

I discovered sunshine was good for the soul. One day, when I was outside walking through the parking lot to my car, a guy about my age in a truck pulled up beside me. I don't know why, but I felt drawn to him, like a good friend. I walked up to his window and he asked me why I was here and I asked him the same. He was there for his grandpa who had raised him. He was in CCU, as well. The guy's name was Tim. He is now my brother. Tim is the best of the best. He was a former motorcycle police officer who happens to have a prosthetic leg, due to someone purposely running over him when he was on duty. Tim is a precious soul and a Godsend. Our family needed him and he needed us. Another gift. Thanks, Lord. Tim was one of the lucky ones like us, he got to leave the hospital with his grandpa, who did end up passing away in the next year or so. We grieved with him. Tim is a husband and a dad. One of the good guys....

Benji and Tim

Davina

July 4th – Davina's email to Benji - Happy 4th of July. We will make up for it next year.

Jodi

July 5th Jodi's Facebook post - Benji update as of this morning:

We are praising the Lord for the fact that he is and has been stable for a couple of days!! Mom says these are MAJOR prayer requests, as decisions will be made later today based on these two situations.

1. INCREASED PLATELET COUNT

2. STAMINA TO BREATHE ON HIS OWN

I have another request for strength and endurance for my parents. They have been at the hospital now for 15 days and I'm sure are exhausted. They are mostly hanging out in the CCU waiting room all the live long day, so you can imagine how tiring that must be. Thank you so much to all of you who have paid them a visit - it really lifts their spirits and keeps them going each day! Also, continue to pray for Davina. Such a hard thing for her as she is missing him so very much. Keep those prayers coming!

Davina

July 6th **Davina's** email to Benji: I hope I'm not boring you with these emails. It's really my only way to communicate with you. I hear you had a good day. Dillon seems pleased with your progress. Sorry I'm not there with you. I went back to work today since they don't want us to over-stimulate you. It was a decent day. Maybe it will last for a bit this time. Love you lots. So glad you are doing better. OXOX

Janelle

They are going to enforce the visitation rules for CCU. I view this as the best news ever! They want you to come out of the coma slowly, with little stimulation. That's just fine with me; I can pray and wait patiently in the waiting room just as well for you to wake up!

They are slowly going to bring him out of the coma.

Jodi

It came to a point at which Benji's doctors and nurses were asking us to have limited visits to his room. Too much stimulation was not good for him at this time. His body needed rest. Because of this, we spent a lot of time in the waiting room. We met so many precious souls who were all in the same place we were, at the point of desperation. And when you're desperate, there's only one place to turn, and it's to the Lord. In the waiting room, we had prayer circles, one-on-one prayers with strangers, and many meaningful conversations. In the waiting room, you can find God. And an *abundance* of love! There are no colors and there are no social statuses, no lines, just people hanging on to hope and sharing hope with each other. Sometimes, when life gets too crazy, I think about those days and how sweet they were. You had no choice but to slow down and notice those around you who were hurting. We should all live life like that a little more often. Look around. Be aware. Love people.

July 7th – Jodi's Facebook post - Update on Benji this morning:

His doctor came in and said she is extremely happy with his progress! Great news to start the day!

Platelets have come up over last 2 days, but would still like to see an increase! Speaking of platelets - Benji's good friend, Dondi Alley Rowe is in the process of setting up a blood drive in Benji's name. More info on this coming soon, so be watching for that!

Overall, he is doing better and better each day. He has made great strides the past 2-3 days especially - he is so strong! Thank you, Lord, for answered prayer

Davina

July 8th –Davina's Facebook post:

I cannot begin to express how thankful I am. Benji Evans developed a very severe case of pancreatitis 3 weeks ago. This morning the physicians removed the ventilator & told us we are turning the corner. Our friends & family have stood strong and prayed continuously. I cannot imagine going through this without your help. Thanks so much for all you have done. God continues to show Himself faithful. Please continue to pray as he continues to heal. Much love.

***

My Awakening

Benji

July 8th, 2016 – I had the weirdest dream I have ever had. For some reason, I felt like I was in a Walgreen's pharmacy in Cushing, Oklahoma, strapped to a gurney, telling the nurse I was in the wrong bed? I have no idea at all why I thought I was in that particular pharmacy, as I have never stepped foot inside it. In reality, what happened was, they had partially taken me out of the coma, but put me back under, to keep from giving me too much stimulation after having been under for 18 days.

When I fully woke up on Friday July 8th, my dad was sitting there (they would only allow one person in at a time at this point) and he started to ask me questions about things that had happened before I got sick. Since I am a big sports fan, he was asking me about the NBA Playoffs, Oklahoma State in the College World Series, and the St. Louis Cardinals. Then he asked me if I knew what today's date was and I told him no. He said it was July 8th and my jaw just dropped and I said, "You have got to be kidding me. I have a catering event for Richard's 90th birthday tomorrow!" (Even though I was a banker full time, I occasionally catered special events.)

With one comment, they felt confident I didn't have any brain damage due to the blood clots. It was a huge relief for everyone to say the least.

Davina

I had managed to find a new routine while Benji was ill. I would drive to the city and stay two days and drive home every third evening. It was my way of recharging. Benji's family found immense comfort in the visitors. They lifted and encouraged them.

We had only been married two-and-a-half years. I was meeting the Evans' family friends daily. And there were so many! To say the Evans family is gregarious may be an understatement; it's part of their charm. But as his wife, I really wanted to wait and grieve in private.

It was difficult to be in Benji's room too much. While he was fighting for his life, with all the machines, tubes and IVs attached, reality was grim. Driving home was my respite.

Benji's team decided to bring him out of sedation

fully on a morning I was in Ponca City. They had been slowly decreasing his sedation over several days. They discontinued the paralytics first. Once sedation was decreased, Benji's eyes were able to focus. I told him I loved him and had missed him. He gave me a thumb's up! It thrilled my heart and gave me comfort. He was still very highly sedated; we were limited to small amounts of time with him, so he wouldn't be over-stimulated. No one really knew the timeline when he would be fully conscious. It just happened to be a morning I was not there.

Once the team brought Benji out of sedation, only one family member at a time was allowed in his room at first. Since I was not there yet, Brad and Janelle decided it would be Brad. When I made it to the waiting room, Brad was back from his visit. The next 30-45 minutes seemed like a lifetime. I hadn't had a conversation with my husband in 18 days, and he was AWAKE just a few rooms away! The nurse, Shawn, finally came back and allowed me in his room.

I took his hand and told him, "Welcome back! Do you know who I am?" He nodded and looked down. I told him I loved him and was so happy he was back. I then told him that I didn't sign up for a three-year marriage; I signed a long-term contract. My Benji-warrior was awake; we were going to be okay!

Davina's Facebook post - Welcome back, love! Nice to catch up with you!

Benji

When Davina got there, the first thing I remember her saying is, "I didn't sign up for a three-year marriage." This was one of the hardest things I have ever been through in my life, up until this point. I knew, when we said our vows at the wedding, we were now together forever but, in this moment, I really understood it was now "US" instead of "She and I." It really was a life-changing moment. From this point forward, I knew I had to get through this for both of us.

Janelle

Words cannot express how happy I was that you were awake, and could talk to us, and we could talk to you! I will sing His praises for the rest of my life. I will be grateful, thankful and blessed for the rest of my life. I will tell the story of Jesus' healing hand and the miracles He performed.

Jodi

After being in a coma for 18 days, the doctors finally decided Benji was ready to come out of it. I could not wait to tell him all the baseball he had missed. It was right during the College World Series! Really, it was the last thing he cared about. I was relieved to know he didn't seem to remember anything. He was oblivious to all the scary things we all had to endure. Thankful.

I began to see a different kind of hope in the doctors' and nurses' eyes. Not so much panic. Instead of saying things like, "He's not out of the woods yet," they began saying things like, "As long as things continue trending upward, he is going to be okay." It was a much better place to be than before. They would tell us his recovery was going to be a *very* long, difficult road. They kept saying this over and over. We would soon find out why.

Jodi's Facebook post – Update on Benji:

Well...today is sort of the day we've been waiting for all this time... Because Benji has been breathing on his own without support from the machine for the past 2 days, they took him off the ventilator this morning and brought him completely out of sedation!!!!! His doctor said WE HAVE TURNED THE COR- NER!!!!! Words cannot express our happiness!!!!!! We can finally communicate with him again!!!

There is no doubt he still has a way to go with his recovery, but we feel like he is definitely on the right track. Oh! And also - his platelets have come up a lot the past 24 hrs! Yay! Praise!!

There is so much power in prayer, and we KNOW you prayed him through this. Please continue to lift him up - he will need to gain lots of strength back. Thank you, thank you, thank you!

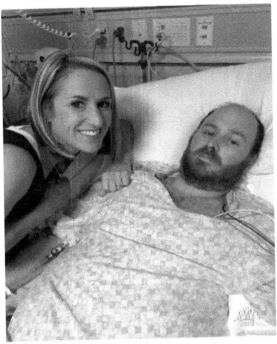

Jodi and Benji on July 11th, 2016 shortly after he came out of the coma.

Dillon

The first day Benji was truly awake, and I had the opportunity to talk with him, was 21 days after the day I was sitting on the beach and found out about him being sick. I got to sit in his room and talk and laugh a bit with him. It was surreal, and so encouraging to see that the Benji we all knew and loved before this was still there. After two more weeks, he was able to leave the hospital and it was nothing short of a miracle; this was a brief shining light and then it seemed like he couldn't catch a break for the next six months.

Janelle

They say it was 18 days that you were in a coma. I can view this time as being the shortest time in my life, or I can view it as the longest time in my life. Either of those can be the truth, at any given time. The nurses almost seemed to want to give us high-fives when we came to visit you. They are *very* proud of the roles they have played in keeping you alive, and they are finding out what kind of person you are. We kept telling them how special you were, and how helpful you have been to others all your life, and now they could see it for themselves!

Davina

July 9th – **Davina's** email to Benji: I don't want to disturb you, but I'm missing you. Looking forward to you coming home. So glad you are sticking around and I'm getting another chance to love you the rest of our days. Love you lots.

Benji

Since coming out of the coma, I have only been allowed to have a few ice chips and a tiny sponge dipped in water that I can suck on. Each time someone new came into my room, I would ask for them to give me more ice chips and water. Dad was really good about telling everyone to limit how much they gave me. Apparently, in the beginning, it isn't good to get much fluid in a person when they have been in a coma for a long time,

My best friend (since the nursery at church) Tyke came to see me today. Dad forgot to mention to him about the ice and the sponge. I kept asking for another spoonful of ice and the chance to suck on the sponge some more. As my best friend, of course he continued to do as I asked. When he left the room, Dad asked if I kept annoying him asking for more ice or for the sponge, because I was begging everyone, and how getting too much could kill me. Tyke just said no. He still gets really mad at me when I bring it up. He thought he might have killed me by giving me too much ice. He doesn't laugh anywhere near as much as I do at the memory.

Jodi

July 10th – Jodi's Facebook post - Update on Benji:

These words are directly from my mom tonight!

We are SO very grateful and thankful for God's healing hand on Benj. He continues to have amazing progress in every way and we love having conversations with him. They continue to decrease meds and his platelet count is now 100,000!! He has a long way to go but he is strong and prepared to do the work necessary. The doctors and nursing staff are all in agreement that he has had mighty miracles blessed upon him. Your prayers made this happen. THANK YOU from the bottom of our hearts. To God Be the Glory!

Davina

July 11th – Davina's email to Benji: Looking forward to seeing you. Hope you rest well tonight. Sweet dreams, love.

Jodi

July 12th – Jodi's Facebook post - Update on Benji:

Things are going very well today! Benji got moved to the 4th floor last night (room 442), which is a lower level of ICU than where he has been the past 3 weeks, yet he still has the benefit of ICU nurses (who we LOVE!!!).

He is feeling good and continues to have less & less tubes. He will actually get to have his first taste of Jello today! He will also start physical therapy and maybe try to walk a little today as well. Great big strides!!

The journey to total wellness will be rather long and probably not really easy. But he is ready to work hard to get there! It has been so fun for us to get to visit with him and share all the stories of the past 23 days. He has enjoyed hearing about all the people who came to visit, called or sent messages asking about him. If he didn't know before, he definitely knows now how much he is loved by so many!! Thank you for the continued prayers and love you have sent his/our way!

Benji

I don't remember who said it during those first days, but I do distinctly remember someone saying, "The doctors didn't know if you were going to make it. God has more for you to do. He isn't done with you yet." The words have stuck with me since that day. I shouldn't have made it. He isn't finished with me. BUT GOD!

Grateful and Thankful!

One of my first full memories of the nurses has to have been the second day out of the coma. I had a NG tube they were using to "feed" me. I have a horrible gag reflex, and it was tickling my throat and I didn't like it one bit. Basically, it was making me gag every few minutes.

The nurse that was there that day (she was a traveling nurse and I hate to admit I don't remember her name) explained to me that she couldn't take it out yet. I explained to her that either she could take it out, or I was going to take it out. It was up to her. She went and found the doctor and brought her back into the room. The doctor explained how I was getting my nutrition from the NG tube and she would like to keep it in for one more day. The nurse told the doctor what I said about pulling it out myself if she didn't take it out. The doctor said that she would let her pull it out, but if I threw up, she was putting it back in, and it was much worse putting it in when you were awake. I told her I wouldn't throw up.

The doctor and nurse just looked at each other with the look that said, "Good luck with that." The nurse pulled the tube out and I gagged as it went through my throat and then was just fine. I felt like I had just conquered the world. I am proud to say, the nurse was impressed that I didn't throw up. Of course, since I hadn't had any real food for over 20 days, there really wasn't anything for me to throw up!

I also remember Pastor Hughes coming to my room multiple times. He told me how his family and my church family had been praying over me. He mentioned how, when he came into my room, he would pray saying, "God, I am not ready to do Benji's funeral." Once again, the prayers warriors kept me going!

July 12ᵗʰ – I was moved to a step-down CCU room. I was also able to eat for the first time since going to the hospital. I ate vegetable broth for the first 24 hours, then I was able to move on to Jell-O. I had been living on IV nutrition for the past few weeks.

You would never believe how good the first bowl of Jell-O tasted! It was green Jell-O. It was a little bit of heaven. I still love that flavor! Believe it or not, the vegetable broth was pretty fantastic as well. I spent a couple of days in the step-down room, then was moved to a regular room. Of course, one of the first things that happened when I got to the regular room was, I had to go to the bathroom. My dad was there and he helped me into the bathroom, and then my sister called. Dad thought I had my balance, but due to my weakness, I fell. You can only guess how that went over with my new nurse. To say she was unhappy I had fallen is definitely an understatement. She ended up being one of the best nurses that I had my entire time in the hospital.

Davina

July 12ᵗʰ – Davina's email to Benji: Life is boring without you.

July 13ᵗʰ – Davina's Facebook post: Perfect day-surprised Benji Evans at the hospital. He is doing AMAZING! Visited with several friends and had a lovely dinner with Dondi. Thankful seems so inadequate. I'm truly blessed beyond measure

July 14ᵗʰ – Davina's Facebook post: Benji Evans continues to improve. Today his doctor told him "he was doing awesome." In the next few days, he will be transferred to the rehab unit & begin physical

& occupational therapy. Fun. Please continue to pray for a speedy recovery; your prayers are working! We are so thankful for the excellent care we have received here at Deaconess.

Janelle

It's July 14 and Jodi's 40th birthday! Jeff has not only "held down the fort" for both him and the kids, but he's put together a surprise birthday party for Jodi in Stephenville. It's the first time we have been away from the hospital since June 19th, so it almost feels "wrong" to leave, but I'm so glad we were able to celebrate with her. I can't say enough how grateful we are that Jeff made it possible for Jodi to be with us at the hospital. I still laugh at the selfie he took, and his saying he had it all under control and not to worry. It was priceless! The picture was of him with a look of pure panic. It was a joke that made us all laugh and we needed humor in the worst way. Jodi was the sunshine for our souls in so many ways, and we are so very grateful she was with us. She never let her joy leave her, but at the same time, she shared it with everyone she met.

Benji

July 15th –There was a blood drive today at RCB Bank where I work. Our great friend Dondi, along with Sandy (who works at the bank), set this up so people could donate blood in my name to help offset some of the costs of the expenses for the blood I received. It was a four-hour blood drive and they actually had to turn people away, because they had so many donors. They took pictures of the donors to give to me for when I come home, and I knew almost all of the donors.

The friends we have in Ponca City have been so caring. There was also a community blood drive that was previously scheduled on July 12th, and there were many people who donated in my name on this day. On August 9th, the Stillwater branch of my bank also had a blood drive. When it was all said and done, I received over 80 credits for people donating in my name. The caring of all the people just continues to amaze me. I had no idea how those people that gave blood in my name would give me a cause that became a very important part of my life. More on this later.

Our neighbors, Mark and Marcy, brought their kids down. I say "kids" but they are all teenagers. The birthday I was supposed to cook for the day after I came out of the coma was for Mark's grandad. They had been in the Dominican Republic when I got sick, and when they got home, Davina told them I wouldn't be able to cook for them. Mark couldn't understand how I wouldn't be able to cook in three weeks.

They had visited while I was in the coma and Mark understood after that. I remember Marcy standing there, holding my hand, crying. She was the first person who had cried around me in the hospital. It was tough seeing how my illness had an effect on other people.

July 16th – I was moved to rehab at Deaconess Hospital. I had lost over thirty pounds (I started at 195) and my muscles had severe atrophy from not being used for the past four weeks. The Physical and Occupational Therapists did everything they could to work me back into shape over the next week, and there were definitely times I did not want to see them.

They pushed me to the point where I thought I would break, then moved me just a little further on. This was exactly what I needed to have happen. I sure didn't enjoy it at the time, but it was exactly what I had to do to get on the way to recovery. It wasn't like I was in the best shape going into the hospital, but after three or four hours in therapy every day, I was absolutely worn out.

I was blessed as Todd, Cindi, and Evan Taylor came to see me while I was in therapy. Cindi is a physical therapist and it was nice having an outside opinion to say they were doing all the exercises she would have had me doing. She did inform me, once I got out, my therapy would not be ending. I had a long way to go to get back to where I was before getting sick.

Davina

July 16th – Davina's Facebook post: Yesterday Benji Evans reached my 1st personal milestone. He was released from the medical unit and readmitted into the Rehab unit. He checked himself into the ER at Ponca City on Father's Day. I wasn't there for that. I was out of town visiting my Dad for the weekend. Saturday morning, I suggested he not make the 3hr trip if he didn't feel like it. He tried to go. We made it as far as Stillwater for lunch before we realized he wasn't up for traveling. He asked a friend to drive him back home & then off I went to Okemah without him.

He had a low-grade fever, nausea, & "some pain." Nothing to be concerned about, I am a pharmacist after all. Sunday morning, I received a text from him saying he went to the ER around midnight. "Ok...so what did they say," I asked. It's either gallstones or pancreatitis, waiting for the doctor to see me. This is Sunday morning at 7:30. "So they admitted you?"

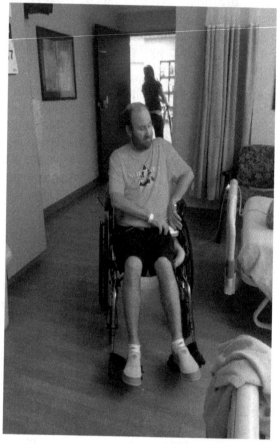

Benji on the first day he moved into the physical therapy and rehab part of the hospital.

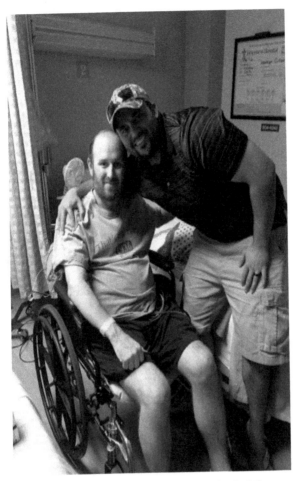

Aaron visiting Benji during his time in physical therapy.

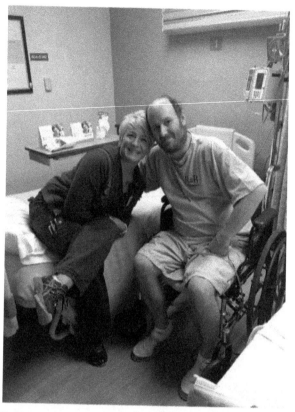

Benji getting to "meet" his new sister Meg after being in physical therapy for a couple of days. Meg was on vacation when he was brought out of the coma.

Janelle

Brad went back to work after Benji was moved to the step-down unit, and I stayed at the little apartment we had rented. The move to the rehab was really a celebration. Even though they really worked him over, at least he had some control over his recovery. But there was so much he had to learn...from using a walker to relearning to walk, climbing stairs, how to cook an egg at the stove without tiring out...so many things to relearn. Progress was being made daily and he was the happiest guy alive when they said he could go home!!

Grateful and Thankful!

Chapter 5

Heading Home

Benji
July 22nd

Since today is my last day in the hospital, I told Mom I wanted to go over to the CCU unit and thank all the nurses for the great work and compassion they had shown. I was able to walk at the time, but it took so much of my energy Mom decided to take me over in a wheelchair. The nurses were so happy to hear I was going home. Dr. O'Neal happened to be in there and came over to talk to me, and when I stood up, he gave me a hug. He said he was so happy I had beaten the odds and was able to go home, and the fact I got out of the wheelchair really surprised him. We wheeled down to the other end to see a nurse down there. Dr. O'Neal came and asked if I wanted to see a picture of what the triglycerides looked like when they took them out. Of course, I wanted to see it, so he took out his phone and started going through pictures. At the time, I didn't think anything about him having a picture on his phone, but after a while, I got to thinking, you know things are pretty bad when the doctors take pictures with their phones! Right before we left, Dr. O'Neal came up and asked if I would answer a medical question for him. He wanted to know if I could remember anything from when I was in a coma. He was happy to hear I didn't remember anything for three weeks.

Davina came down with our neighbors, Mark and Marcy Cross, to take me home from rehab. I had been in the hospital for 35 days. It was definitely a great milestone in my recovery and I was so happy to be on my way back home. I had to use a walker when I got home, because I was so weak, but being home was all that mattered.

I do have to say the nurses told me how the Evans family completely took over the waiting room at the CCU unit. I don't know how many visitors came by to see us, but it was in the hundreds for sure. We received so many get well cards, prayers, plants, and flowers it would be impossible to count. I even received over a dozen cards from people I didn't know, but who attended a church in Alabama that a family friend attends. It was such a blessing to receive prayers from people I didn't even know. The funniest thing I received was when Aaron brought me ammunition to physical therapy as a get-well gift. I laughed so hard at this, because they would have kicked me out if they'd found it!

Roy Wile literally came to the hospital every single day to check in on my family, and his wife, Ruby, picked up my parents' dirty clothes to wash them every few days. They had only brought clothes for a couple of days, because they hadn't planned to be there for a month. "Thank you" will never be enough for all of the kindness shown by so many people.

My mom was literally by my side all but three of those first 35 days. She left on Friday, July 14th to celebrate my sisters 40th birthday and came back on Sunday. I was so blessed to always have someone there when I needed them. I was even able to "meet" my nurse Meg while in therapy. It was great meeting someone I had heard so much about.

Janelle

For the first time since June 18th, all our family was just where they should be: Benji and Davina are at their home in Ponca City, Jeff and Jodi are loving on their kids in Stephenville, and Brad and I are unpacking in Cleburne. We knew it would be a long recovery, because over and over they told us that, but we didn't have a clue how difficult the recovery would be in the coming months.

Grateful and Thankful!

Jodi

July 22nd – Jodi's Facebook Post: Today is a day to celebrate! Benji, I am so proud of you and all the hard work you've put in the last couple of weeks to get better! God's not done with you yet! This is the song that gave me comfort when you were not doing well & I believed and held on to these lyrics. So thankful for your life! #ourGodisgreater #ourGodisHealer

Benji

July 25th – I called Blake Vowel today to tell him how happy I was to have had him as the paramedic on my flight. Even though I don't really remember the flight, I do know it was calming having someone I knew very well to talk with. When I told him how I felt that he saved my life by giving me just a bit of water, he said he had to find something for me to drink because he thought it was a dying man's last request. He said there was no way his last memory of me was going to be him saying no to this request. In the condition I was in, he knew the little bit of water he gave me wasn't going to kill me. He thought, with everything going on, I wasn't going to make it with or without the water. I knew how bad things had been before he said this but hearing it from a friend who sees the worst of injuries as a flight paramedic really drove it home.

Davina Evans is with **Jodi Evans Weyers** and 3 others. ···

Jul 26, 2016 · 👥

After a 35 day hospital stay, I was finally able to bring Benji Evans home! 🐿 We are so very thankful that God intervened & gave us more time together . Benji developed pancreatitis triggered by sudden elevated triglyceride levels.

He essentially defied every odd stacked against him–& there were many! He was on the ventilator ~21 days. Not only was he in a medically induced coma, he was on paralytics so that he could not disrupt his open incision site. He was very critical most of his stay. Science told us we could lose him at any moment. His physician initially did not expect him to make it. BUT GOD!

We are humbled at the outpouring of support from our community, friends, & family. Your support & prayers held us when when all I could do was stand (or at times-crumble)on God's promises. We can finally begin to heal together. 💟 Please continue to pray for us during our time of recovery. Love & hugs.

July 26th – Davina Facebook post

***

Back to Deaconess

Benji

July 30th – I continued my physical therapy at the Ponca hospital just a couple of days after getting home. I also had a wound-vac machine I had to carry to continue getting out the fluids my pancreas was excreting in my abdomen. Basically, it was a suction pump with a hose that went inside my abdomen. The physical therapists also had to change out the dressing around that tube. Pulling the tape off was brutal each and every time.

I had been home for nine days but had been feeling just a bit "off" for the past couple of days, with a fever that just continued to increase. Tonight, it was over 103 and I called Dillon to get his opinion about what to do. He said to head to the ER. Davina loaded me up and took me to the ER here in Ponca. We discussed everything that had happened over the past six weeks with the doctor, and he decided I needed to go back to Deaconess in Oklahoma City.

Davina ran home to grab some clothes and got back just as I was about ready to get loaded into the ambulance. They got me there as soon as they could (sometime around midnight), and I was admitted to the ER. I stayed there for a couple of hours as they ran more blood work and a CT scan to figure out what was causing the fever. One of the weird things that started to happen was that fluid started coming out around the tube in my abdomen. It literally looked like I had wet the bed. It would be months before that would be finished. Eventually, they moved me to a regular room which happened to be the same room I was in before I started the physical therapy.

One thing I did find kind of funny about going back to the hospital was, the next morning I woke up and they brought me mail. The hospital had received more cards for me during the nine days I was home. They just hadn't sent them on to me yet, so I was fortunate to have a handful of get-well cards waiting on me when I got to the hospital. It was a really nice thing to have the words of encouragement on my first day back. I had a good laugh with the nurses about it.

Before going to the hospital, I had posted on Facebook asking if any of my friends would be willing to mow our yard. Our neighbor, Chuck, had mowed it every week since I had gotten sick. He was happy to continue doing it, but I felt guilty having him do it every week. Within a couple of hours, I had it set up for the next month to have a different person come and mow. If you are a person who enjoys mowing and know someone is in the hospital, take your mower over and just do it. It was truly another huge blessing not having to worry about the yard being three feet tall. I asked again at the end of August about people mowing in September and it was the exact same response. I was turning people away who wanted to help.

I ended up meeting with three different doctors the next day (two of whom I had met before) and they told me I had a pseudocyst (when a pancreas is injured, sometimes the ducts become blocked and can form a fluid filled sac) that had formed around my pancreas; there was some type of infection. They took me to surgery and inserted a small drain to try to get rid of the fluid. They begin running tests to find out what type of infection I had, so they could give me an antibiotic to clear it up. It took much longer than we had hoped to figure out what the infection was, but they did decide on a strong "cocktail" of antibiotics to get me back to healing.

The best news during this time was the Summer Olympics in Rio were going on, so I was able to watch this throughout the day and night to keep me from going completely insane.

One issue that began to show up during this time was that my skin (and whites of my eyes) began to turn yellow. It was jaundice. It really started to look like I was glowing, and the doctor explained my bilirubin was high and they needed to do a procedure called an ERCP to open the bile duct in my liver to allow the fluid to drain. This was another bump in the road but it had to be done.

The doctor attempted the procedure, but it was not successful. This was really a downer for us, because we knew it was something that had to be fixed. He said he just couldn't get through the tubes to get in to open the duct.

Davina

August 4th – Davina's email to Benji: Good morning, love. Slept well. Woke up a couple times but was able to go back to sleep. Gizmo (our Shih Tzu) slept on the bed last night. I guess he has forgiven me for taking away his jerky! Lucia (our cat) is more affectionate than ever. I'm going to work today. It will be good to be back. I did need yesterday to rest but am feeling better today. Hope you were able to get some rest. Praying you have less pain today....

August 6th – Davina's Facebook post: Successful attempt to recharge after the last 8 weeks. Our lives will never be the same, but that doesn't mean it won't be better! I am reminded of Mother Teresa's 'God won't give me anything I can't handle but I wish He didn't trust me so much'.... I am so very thankful. My heart is full.

August 7th – Davina's email to Benji: I'm missing you tonight. No one is asking me to turn down my music and I have all the remotes on my side. That's actually a good thing though. While I've wanted to be with you before, or I've worried about you, I have been too emotionally spent to actually miss you. This means I, too, am healing. I love you more than I know how to say. Thanks for sticking around for me.

August 8th – **Davina's** email to Benji: Looking forward to you coming home or at the very least, talking to you tomorrow night. I know neither of us enjoys spending a lot of time on the phone but I enjoy hearing your voice.

August 10th – **Davina's** email to Benji: I had 3 people ask about you today. Believing for a good report tomorrow...ready for you to come home. Love you, mean it.

Benji

August 11th – They did another CT scan and found another fluid build-up the drain cannot reach. They decided they will operate on Monday the 15th to insert a larger drain (about the size of my pinkie).

Janelle

To be honest, I don't know how many trips to OKC we made after Davina made the CALL to us that Benji was going back to the hospital –again. I just know the apartment complex we stayed in had made sure an apartment was always available, just in case it was needed. I only had to make a call on the way to OKC and they handled everything for me. and assured me he would be lifted up in prayer. Each time we saw him, he was losing more and more weight. With the jaundice turning his skin and eyes bright yellow, it was difficult to see how he was on the road to recovery.

Dillon

I got the phone call that Benji was back in in the Oklahoma City hospital. He still had multiple complications stemming from his severe case of pancreatitis. He had developed a large pseudocyst around his pancreas, which was a collection of fluid that was walled up in his abdomen. This was large enough to have caused an obstruction of the bile trying to leave his liver, and he became severely jaundiced.

My wife had come to sit with me, family, and friends in the waiting room several times over the first hospital stay, but she never went back to Benji's room. When he was re-admitted, one of the next few times, she went with me to visit. I warned her he didn't look good, but upon leaving to head home after a great visit, she chastised me for failing to adequately explain and prepare her for the shock of seeing him the first time. He had lost about 40 pounds on his 5ft 8in frame, his stomach was severely distended from the fluid build-up, he could barely walk, and then only a few feet, and his skin was a bright neon yellow. He scarcely looked like the person we knew.

Soon after, I took care of a patient in the ER where I worked who was dying from stomach cancer. He was about Benji's and my same age and only had a few weeks left to live. I remember thinking how he physically looked the same as Benji. Both were extremely thin, frail, jaundiced, and had extreme fluid build-up in the abdomen. I had trouble focusing on what he was saying, because I couldn't get Benji out of my head. I was still scared he wasn't going to pull through this.

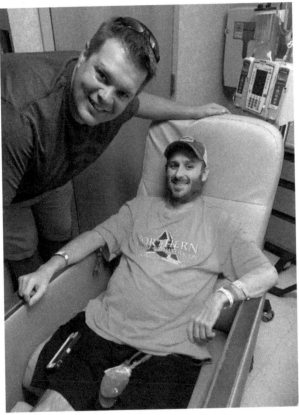

Dillon visiting Benji during his second stay at Deaconess on August 19th, 2016.

Davina Evans was with **Jodi Evans Weyers** and **5 others.**
August 13, 2016 ·

#prayforbenji Update on **Benji Evans**. 2 weeks ago Benji had a high fever & just didn't feel well. I could tell something was wrong so we went to the ER here in Ponca. They ran tests & the CT scan showed a fluid body near his pancreas. They transferred him via ambulance to Deaconess where his team of doctors are.

The radiologist drew cultures & place a drain in the fluid body. They also began antibiotic treatment. Over the past 2 weeks, the drain worked well. Thursday they repeated the CT to find there is another fluid body above his pancreas that the drain cannot reach.

Monday morning at 7:30, they are taking Benji to surgery to remove the fluid, clean up the area, and place another drain that can reach this area. One of his doctors told me that "we need one more miracle"! God has heard every prayer that has been prayed over the past 9 weeks. Please continue to lift us, the physicians & staff, & his family up to the Lord.

God has carried us this far. He will not drop us now.

Thanks so much for ALL YOU HAVE DONE! 🍃

👍😊😮 188   131 Comments   15 Shares

August 13th – Davina Facebook post

Benji

August 15th: For the first time in a few weeks, they brought us good news. They were able to remove the fluid from the "new" pocket, and also removed some parts of the pancreas which were necrotic (dead). This has been very difficult for me, because I was literally sitting around all day doing nothing. I had lost around 40 pounds by this time, and was very weak. I was able to walk without the aid of a walker, but could only go for about five minutes before I had to take a break.

One of the visitors during this time was Bryan and his dad "Pops," who came by on their way from Ponca City back to Houston. It was great talking to them about hunting, and they offered to take me out when I was out of the hospital. I knew there was a lot of work to do before I could get out into the woods, but I was definitely looking forward to going with them.

During this time, I definitely was starting to become agitated, due to having more bad than good happening with my recovery. There is no doubt I was not being the model patient at times. All the people coming to visit were absolutely great, but I was definitely starting to get stir crazy. I don't ever remember asking God, "Why me?" during this time. My issues were more along the lines of, "Why can't all these doctors figure anything out?" Since my doctors were only there early in the morning, they never saw me get out of bed. They asked the physical therapists to come by and make me get up and walk. I was getting up multiple times each day to go to the vending machine or just to go to the bathroom, but they just didn't see it. Being the ornery person I am, a prank needed to be played. The therapist helped me stand up using the walker as support. I slowly walked to the door and turned into the hall. I then put one finger on each side of the walker and took off at a fast pace down the hall. When I got to the end, I asked them if they wanted to make the full circle or if that was good enough. They were really surprised that I wasn't having any kind of issue, because of the doctor's notes. Every couple of days they would come by and make me walk around with them.

One day Jodi and Reese came up to visit and the nurse allowed me to go outside with them in a wheelchair. It was so good to see the sunshine! The next day, they were going to come back to see me, but Reese had come down with a fever. There is no doubt I was a little bit upset that they had come to visit with

Reese getting a fever, but I know the last thing they wanted was for me to get sick from her.

Getting outside for just an hour just made me want to get out more often. A couple of days later, I finally was able to talk my nurse into unplugging me from everything and letting me go outside for an hour and sit right outside the hospital entrance. She made me promise I would come back, because if I didn't, she would lose her job. I asked her where she thought I would be going in a wheelchair; she had a huge look of relief on her face when I came back.

August 22nd – Benji's Facebook post: So after having spent almost 60 days in the hospital since Father's Day (hopefully going home soon), I have lost around 40 pounds. Basically, I have lost almost 1/4 of my body weight. Davina keeps telling me there are cheaper diets I could have gone on. Davina didn't quite see the humor that I did when I told everyone that I was on a new weight-loss program: The Deaconess Diet, with 18 days in a coma guaranteed to shed the pounds. I am fortunate to have kept my sense of humor through most of my issues. Hopefully I will be able to start gaining strength back soon when I am able to leave the hospital again.

August 25th After 25 days in the hospital this time, I am finally headed back home. I have been in the hospital 60 of the last 69 days and it has not been easy. I am ready to be home and stay there. There is no doubt there are more hospital visits to come, but for now, I am headed home.

When I got home, my co-workers had made me a huge sign with words of prayer and support. It was another great showing of care and compassion from my work family.

Davina

August 26th – Davina's Facebook post: After 60 days of inpatient hospitalization, Benji came home yesterday! He survived a life-threatening episode of pancreatitis. Benji defied odds after odds & according to his physician, "it was only by the grace of God he is alive." During this time our support system stood strong. We continue to be humbled at the outpouring of love & prayer from our family, friends, & community. We would not have survived this without your help. We love & appreciate all of you more than we can say. God has directed our steps to an amazing community. Thank you, Ponca City, for showing up so strong for us. Please continue to pray for God's perfect will for our lives. Thanks again for all you do.

Benji

September 3rd – I had a customer post on my Facebook about her looking at a new Camaro. We had been talking about her getting one before I got sick. I said how I thought I would be able to return back to work sometime in October. I had no idea my banking career was now over, and I would not be able to get back to work for almost a year and a half. I thought I would be able to just bounce right back.

Davina Evans is with **Aaron Ghaemi** and **Benji Evans.**

Nov 19, 2016 · Ponca City · 👥

Happy hunting to the Motley Crew- Bryan Robertson Aaron Ghaemi Spencer Grace Benji Evans Benji is sitting this one out but is with you in spirit. When Benji built the shop designed for cleaning & processing his game, I really had no idea it would become 'deer camp'! He took a week off work last year & hunt from sunup to sundown! I would peek my head in, say hello to all the guys, & escape to the house!

The brotherhood they have (& others) is rare but true. So happy you are in our lives! Lindsay Grace

🔵 Jodi Evans Weyers and 53 others   2 Shares

👍 Like   💬 Comment   ↗ Share

November 19th - Davina Facebook post showing Benji at lunch with Aaron and Spencer between hospital stays.

94

Benji

September 12th – Today they are doing an outpatient ERCP. This is to try to open up the common bile duct to allow the fluid to leave my liver. This will get rid of the jaundice. I am so yellow I am pretty much glowing.

Davina

Davina's Facebook post: Please say a prayer for Benji Evans today. He is having an outpatient procedure in OKC. Pray for divine wisdom & direction for the physician & staff. Pray for COMPLETE HEALING for Benji. By HIS stripes WE ARE HEALED. We thank & praise God in advance!

Love you all.

Davina's Facebook post:

Prayer request update - Benji's procedure was unsuccessful. The goal was to open the common bile duct & allow his bilirubin level to normalize. But the GI physician was unable to place the stent in the right area. So we are back to the drawing board for the next plan of action. The good news is Benji is regaining strength (& his charming personality) each day. His initial surgery incision has healed. The first drain is no longer draining so we believe it has done its job! We cherish your prayers; they are working & continue to carry us. God's ways are so much higher than ours. Pray God lights our path. We desire His perfect will every step of the way.

Benji

September 14th – For anyone from a small town, you know how important a county fair can be. I was able to go today and eat some of the yummy (unhealthy) food. Going to "the fair" is kind of like homecoming in September. People come home just to walk around and see everyone. It isn't a very big fair, but Davina always gets frustrated because I can't walk 10 steps without talking to someone I know.

That was not the case this year. I had lost over 50 pounds, and only two people recognized me without hearing my voice. Jackie Steffen, when I walked up to her and asked if she knew who I was, said, "You look a lot like Benji Evans, but there is no way it is you." She couldn't believe what I looked like. Greg Scheu-ermann came up and asked how I was doing. He is the only person who knew who I was when he saw me. With everyone else, I had to say something to them before they recognized me.

My favorite story of the night was when one of my customers sat down next to me. I told him who I was and he looked at me like I was an alien. It was really kind of funny because he just kept saying there is no way it was me. It was at this point I really started to see how much I had changed since June. This was a guy I sat across a desk from every few weeks and he couldn't believe it was the same person. It was kind of a creepy feeling, to be honest.

With regard to September 18th and Davina's Face-book post: As Davina Evans posted last week, the procedure to put the stent in my bile duct was not successful. I am going to be in OKC on Tuesday to meet with my surgeon who is going to remove the small drain tube that I have had since the first week in August to drain an abscess. The larger tube will be kept in.

On Wednesday I am meeting with a surgeon/pancreas specialist at OU Medical Center. This doctor is one of the best in the country when it comes to the pancreas. He comes highly recommended by two friends that are doctors. I am very fortunate to have gotten in to see him this week, as he is very difficult to get in to see.

Please continue to keep my entire family in your thoughts and prayers

September 20th – Benji's Facebook post:

In sickness and in health, till death do us part... These words have taken on a whole new meaning this summer. When I woke up from my coma, Davina said she didn't sign up for a three-year marriage. Well, today is officially three years and I can't thank her enough for taking those words so seriously in the past three months.

You were by my side in the hospital and continue to be, each and every day. Not only are you my wife and pharmacist, but also my nurse, cleaning lady, psychiatrist, and my biggest cheerleader. I will never be able to thank you enough for all you have done over this past summer. I can't imagine you not being by my side through these hard times. Happy Anniversary!

Janelle

Today I celebrate Davina! Today, I thank God for sending you to love our son. Those were the words I told her in a phone call on this day...and those are words that will always be true. Davina's faith, love of God, and love of Benji were all things that lifted the rest of us when we felt discouraged. Happy Anniversary, today and always!

Grateful and Thankful!

Chapter 6

New Hospital and New Doctors

Some background about how I came to OU Medical Center is important here. Bill Rodgers, who was the owner of the first bank my dad worked for, called him after seeing the Facebook post on September 12th. Bill said he'd seen that my second ERCP failed. He knew a ton of doctors in the Oklahoma City area, including his daughter-in-law's father, who was a retired doctor. He asked Dad if he would be offended if he called around to see if there was another doctor who could maybe do the ERCP and have more success.

Bill was not saying anything negative about Deaconess Hospital or the physicians there; he just wanted to help if he could. As a concerned father, of course my dad said we would be grateful for any help we could get. The next day, Bill emailed Dad with contact information and an appointment on September 21st with Dr. Postier, who is the Head of Surgery at OU Medical Center.

The email had the phone and fax number of the office, with a note to call to find out exactly what information they needed. I called his office, explained who I was, and said an appointment had been made for me to see Dr. Postier the next week. The lady I was talking to said she didn't have me in the computer and asked when that appointment had been made. I told her it had been made the day before, and she said something along the lines of, "You don't get in to see Dr. Postier a week after making an appointment." I asked her what information she would need for a new patient and said I was going to send it over and would see her next week. The issue with the appointment not being in the computer was because Dr. Postier was in China giving a speech. The appointment was set up through his personal assistant, not through the clinic.

Facebook was such an important avenue for us, from getting in to see Dr. Postier, to just keeping people informed of the ups and downs. This was a great venue for people to see what was happening and to show us support. I am not a person who posts too many things about my personal life, but in this case, it was a huge blessing to me. I am so grateful to have had a way to keep everyone informed and to have had a place for people to say they were praying for me.

September 21st: I showed up at Dr. Postier's office for my appointment. When I told the receptionist my name, she kind of shook her head, smiled, and told me, "I don't know who you are, but people just don't see the doctor on short notice like this." I told her that I was nobody important, but I knew people who had the correct contacts. At the time, I really had no idea how big of a deal this was. I definitely found out later how people across the state know and respect Dr. Postier. For those of you who don't know, the University of Oklahoma colors are crimson and cream. As an Oklahoma State University graduate, I had to wear my orange shirt for my first visit. When he walked into the room, it was like we had known each other forever and of course he asked about my shirt and told me he was an Oklahoma State graduate, as well. We talked about ten minutes about the football team, and he even showed me a recent picture of his wife with Barry Sanders. It was so nice to meet a doctor for the first time who had a really good personality to go along with his skills. Dr. O'Neal had this same gift. Dr. Postier informed me he had reviewed my files and wanted to refer me to Dr. Maple at OU to work on my pancreas. He was more concerned about my jaundice and said they would attempt to do another ERCP as soon as they could. He called Dr. Maple before I even left the office to explain the issues I was having, to let him know he would be sending him my file, and to see what he could do to fit me in as soon as possible.

One thing Dr. Postier did say was that I should have been at OU from the start, because as a teaching hospital, they had more specialists and the newest equipment. The Ponca hospital had wanted to send me there originally, but they didn't have a bed available.

Then I asked when they would have taken me? When I was in cardiac arrest? When my blood was clotting? When I was in the coma? I explained to him how everything the doctors had done at Deaconess had kept me alive. So, I wasn't sure how OU could have done a better job at this point. I said I was here now for a specialist but I wouldn't have traded being at Deaconess for anything. The doctors and nurses did everything they could to keep me going; I didn't know if I would have gotten the personalized care at OU when I needed it the most.

September 22nd: I received a call at around 10:00 this morning from Dr. Maple's office, and they want me back in Oklahoma City today for another CT scan at 1:30 pm. This didn't give me a whole lot of time, because it is about an hour and a half drive, and I was actually still in bed. (I was sleeping 12-14 hours per day at this time.) They also said they would be doing the ERCP the next day, and I would be receiving a call from the surgery center that afternoon to schedule the time. Within 15 minutes, I received the call from the surgery center, saying they had me scheduled for 1:30 pm Friday the 23rd.

I hadn't even met my new doctors and they were scheduling surgeries. To say things were moving fast was an understatement. This is when I really started to figure out how big of a stick Dr. Postier really carried. I called Davina as I was getting dressed and told her I was heading back to OKC and a surgery was planned for the next day. After getting the CT scan, I went to Dillon and Laura's house in Edmond to spend the night, because there was no reason to make the drive home just to turn around and drive back the next day. I received a call at 5:45 pm from the surgery center saying Dr. Maple had reviewed the CT scan (less than 3 hours after completion) and they were going to postpone the surgery until Monday the 26th, because he wanted to do the ERCP as well as a cyst gastrostomy (basically this is a stent that allows the fluid to drain from the pseudocyst to the stomach). They couldn't fit both procedures into the schedule the next day. I went home and spent the weekend with Davina, praying the surgery would work on Monday.

***

Staying in The Hospital Again?

Davina

September 26th – Davina's Facebook post: #prayforbenji We are requesting prayers once again for Benji Evans. He is having 2 procedures this after-noon to resolve his elevated bilirubin & to drain fluid from the abscess near his pancreas. We are now at OU Medical Center under the care of elite experts in the field. Please pray for divine wisdom to guide the physicians & staff. Pray for ABSOLUTE HEALING for Benji. BY HIS STRIPES WE ARE HEALED!

As one of our friends recently said, "Prayer works, especially in large numbers!" There is no doubt without God's intervention early in this journey; I would be traveling without my husband. We cherish your continued prayers. I trust the God that brought us together to keep us together! Many blessings.

Benji

Once again, the ERCP failed, which was very disap-pointing. They said it just wasn't possible to get to the spot they needed to make it a success. We did have some success though, as Dr. Maple was able to put in the stent from the pseudocyst to my stomach, and went in with his net, grabber and claw (his words not mine) and did a debridement (removal of dead tissue) of what he believed to be 20% of the necrotic pancreas. Due to the ERCP not working again, they decided to admit me into the hospital for a couple of days. This was definitely not in my plans.

Davina

Davina's Facebook post, Benji-Warrior News: The two-fold procedure was half successful. They were unable to get to the bile duct due to excess sludge & compression. The next step is to go through his liver

103

via interventional radiology. This will relieve pressure & allow the bile acid to flow again. If scheduling allows, they will do this tomorrow. They also plan on removing a drain that has served its purpose. The physician was in awe that Benji has been tolerating an oral diet. He said that most in his condition would require a feeding tube or perinatal nutrition. This is a huge blessing we didn't even realize we had! Thanks for your prayers. They are working. God is faithful.

Benji

September 27th: My parents came up for the surgery and we met Dr. Hancock, who was an interventional radiologist. He would be inserting another small drain tube in my liver to drain the fluid that has been building up and causing the jaundice. Basically, I was changing out one drain for the one that was in the pseudocyst that was no longer draining. I also still had the large drain on the left side of my body. I will say Dr. Hancock did a phenomenal job of dumbing this down for us to understand. He took out a piece of paper and drew a liver on it, then showed us where the block was located and explained how he was going to install the drain to get rid of the bile. This was really nice, because we really were using the internet to try to understand everything that was happening, and you know: "They can't put anything on the internet that isn't true!"

Tomorrow Dr. Maple will be going back in for another debridement. It is really a fairly simple process for me as they put me under anesthesia and then I wake up with a sore throat. They will be doing more of these in the future, but they will all hopefully be outpatient procedures. I will just have to get a ride down and back to and from Oklahoma City.

Davina

Davina's Facebook post, Update: today was a happy day! The physician was able to place the drain via interventional radiology on his first attempt. He was very pleased! Also, the original drain placed in August was removed! At least Benji was able to exchange one drain for another! We are unsure of the next course of action. He could be discharged tomorrow. The GI physician told us yesterday he would start to improve a little each day. He did say it would likely take 7-10 days before Benji's yellow hue would resolve itself. Happy to be on the road to resolution.

Dillon

Benji was able to get in to see a great gastroenterologist at University of Oklahoma Medical Center. They were able to place a drain that started draining the built-up bile. This step improved his skin so he wasn't bright yellow.

Benji

I explained to my medical team in the hospital (not my surgeons) that tomorrow was Davina's birthday and mine was on Thursday and I really would like to be home to celebrate with her. It didn't get me out of the hospital any quicker, but the medical team (a doctor, resident, two 4th year med students, two 3rd year med students, and a pharmacist) did bring me a couple of key lime pies and a card for my birthday. It really made me feel like they cared when they did those little things. The drain was working great and I was getting out up to four liters of fluid per day out (more on this coming up). I ended up being released on September 29th, which did happen to be my birthday. My parents drove me back to Ponca City and then headed back to Texas.

Janelle

Best day ever! We got to spend the day with Benji on his birthday, drive him home to his wife, and go home. All is well...everyone is where they should be.

Grateful and Thankful

Davina

September 29th –Davina's Facebook post: Benji was discharged home today! His color has significantly improved. I truly feel he is now on the path to mend! He is tired & in some pain but otherwise doing well. Now we will work on regaining strength. We appreciate every prayer & encouraging word more than we can say!

Benji

I am pretty sure I had more posts on my Facebook today wishing me Happy Birthday than I ever have had. I had over 160 people post. There is no doubt most of those people were the ones praying for me. Once again, this was a great time to have social media.

***

Finally Home… Or Not?

Benji

September 30th – Davina and I were getting ready for bed, but all of a sudden, my hands started to cramp up. I drank a large PowerAde, as well as some water, and she went to get me some potassium pills to help make the cramps go away. Then I threw up two times. So… Back to the Ponca ER we went. They ran some IV's, loaded me up with fluids, and admitted me to the hospital for dehydration.

This was 100% my own fault. I had found a way to squeeze my abdomen to make the fluid drain quicker. That was why I was getting so much out per day. I found out the hard way, if you are getting four liters of fluid out of a drain, you actually have to replace it by drinking more than four liters of fluid. Who would have guessed?

I was released again on October 2nd and the hospitalist Dr. Kasper, whom I have known for over half my life, told me I could continue to get outpatient IV fluids if the drain continued to pull as much fluid as it had been. I did go and get fluids a couple of times over the next few weeks. It was kind of like a pick-me-up for a couple of days.

Davina

October 1st – Davina's Facebook post: The last 3 months have brought so many challenges. In June, my 35-yr. old husband went to bed feeling just fine Friday night & woke up Saturday morning to "my stomach is just off." It was Father's Day weekend &

we were planning to visit my parents in Okemah. Benji decided not to go. In typical Benji-style, he wanted me to go & enjoy time with my Dad. He went to the ER that night knowing something was very wrong. We had no idea just how wrong things were. He had pancreatitis complicated by diabetes. He was life-flighted out Sunday evening to OKC & went into cardiac arrest around 3 am Monday morning. The physician told me that if things continued to trend the way they were, he would not make it. He kindly suggested I call his family...thus our saga began. I now realize how much I needed the foundation my parents had established at an early age. I was taught the power of prayer as a very young girl. During those difficult days, I remembered this ..."Perhaps this is the very moment for which you were created!" (Ester 4:14). The hand of God was so very evident. The physician noted in Benji's medical records that it is 'only by the grace of God he is alive.' I am so very thankful for God's mercy & grace. It is new every morning; we have used it each & every day! God's ways are so much higher than our ways. I would have never asked for this, but God has allowed it & is bringing us through stronger than ever. No matter what you are going through, rely on the Lord. Trust in the Lord with all your heart. He will never leave you! I pray our story has encouraged & strengthened your day!

Benji

October 3rd: Last night I was in bed and my lower back was absolutely killing me. I decided to move out into the recliner, where I was able to sleep for a few hours. I woke up to a severe pain where the small drain was located to drain the bile from my liver. There was very little fluid in the bag, which didn't make sense to me, because there had been quite a bit of fluid up until this time.

I went and laid down in the bed for a couple more hours while Davina was at work and by 11:30 am. the bag was full (approx. one liter). By 2:00 pm, the bag was full again, so I now had some concerns I might get dehydrated again. I was drinking lots of fluids.

October 6th: I went back today for another debridement of the pseudocyst by Dr. Maple. The procedure lasted over two hours and he thinks he was able to get most of the necrotic tissue. He wanted me to get another CT scan next week to see the progress. He also thought the bile duct was now open and believed the fluid would move through like it was supposed to, so we could maybe cap the drain tube. Still, he wanted to check with Dr. Hancock to confirm. This would be a phenomenal thing to have happen, because carrying around a drain bag has not been a fun thing, to say the least.

Oct 11th: I did the CT scan today that Dr. Maple had requested. They will get back to me next week to see if they need to go back in again. Of course, I am hoping it will just be one more time.

Davina

Oct 21st – Davina's Facebook post: Today was a good day. It was a very 'normal' day filled with typical life issues and a few atypical blessings -and for that I am thankful!

Benji

Oct 22nd: Aaron came up and helped me set up a deer blind. Davina has some pretty strict rules for me about hunting, and Aaron is happy to make sure I follow all of them. No climbing trees, can't hunt while on blood thinners, can't drag a deer, and can't use a knife. We had a deer come up about 15 yards and I just watched her, with Aaron telling me to take the shot. I was enjoying watching all of the wildlife so much I just couldn't bring myself to shoot.

When you pull the trigger, this is when the real work begins and I was just happy to be outside and just watching the deer, coyotes and squirrels, without worrying about pulling the trigger. We went another time, and didn't see anything, but it didn't matter to me at all. I was just enjoying the nature God had given us.

This same week, I called one of my customers and good friends, Justin Sober. I asked if I could hunt out at his place. He was happy I wanted to go, and hesitantly asked me if I wanted to hunt alone, or if I would be willing to have him hunt with me. For anyone who enjoys the outdoors, you understand what he was saying. I just wanted to get outside and do something I love, and he didn't want to interrupt it. Of course, I was excited to spend time with a friend in the woods.

During the next week we were able to go out two different times. He was able to just drive me right up to the blind and wouldn't even let me haul my gear in. Justin had let me hunt before, and we had an agreement on the type of deer I could shoot. Of course, with my illness, he threw that all out the window and wanted me to shoot the first one we saw. We saw deer both times, but I was just enjoying watching them; once again, I never pulled the trigger. All I wanted was to be out in the woods hunting, which has been a passion of mine since I was a very small child. I will never be able to thank these guys enough for taking me out to do one of the things I dearly love.

Oct 28th: Today Dr. Maple went in and did another debridement. He still wasn't able to get all of it. I was really hoping this would have been the final time, so it was a bit of a letdown, but we will continue to do as he says; we'll know each time he goes in, there will be less necrotic tissue than before. I was able to meet with a nurse from interventional radiology, and she gave me plugs for the small drain in my liver, because it really hadn't been draining much over the past couple of weeks.

I no longer have to carry around the large drain bag, which is definitely a good thing. They are planning to remove the drain or internalize it (still no clue how this really works) on November 8th. On Halloween, I received a call from Dr. Maple's office and they were trying to work with interventional radiology to schedule a time to remove the drain and do another debridement on November 14th so I don't have to make two trips. I really am grateful they do work together to make it easier on the patient.

The large drain in the pseudocyst is really annoying and at times painful, so I am REALLY hoping it will be removed during this next procedure.

Chapter 7

The Bleed

Benji
November 11th:

This morning, I woke up while Davina was getting ready. This pretty much never happens. As we were talking, I told her I felt like I was going to be sick, so she got me a bag. I threw up and told her I must have bitten my tongue, because I tasted blood. She asked if I bit my tongue or if I threw up blood, and I said I had no idea.

She turned on the light and I looked down and saw I had thrown up over a liter of blood. This was definitely a new thing to us and was shocking to say the least. She asked me if I could make it to the car to take me back to the ER. I told her I could not and she needed to call an ambulance. As she was calling the ambulance, I decided I needed to use the bathroom before they got there. At this time, I was so weak I couldn't even stand up to use the bathroom. As I did stand up, I fell flat on my face.

The paramedics showed up, helped get me up, and walked me to the gurney; they loaded me up in the ambulance. On the way to the hospital, I threw up more blood. They gave me blood while in the ER, and told me they were going to fly me back to Deaconess. I explained how I had been going to OU Medical Center; that was where my surgeon was located. The doctor told me OU was currently on divert, which meant they didn't have a room in the ICU for new patients.

I told Davina to go home and get my folder and call Dr. Maples' nurse Janet. The ER doctor said, in 12 years he had never seen a hospital change their mind. Davina came back after calling Janet. The doctor walked in and said, "I have never seen it and don't know who you called, but you are going to OU." Apparently, Dr. Maple carried a pretty big stick, as well. They loaded me up for my second helicopter flight in the past few months, and flew me to OU, where I was admitted into their ICU.

Janelle

Once again, Davina made the CALL to us that Benji was being life-flighted to OU Medical Center because of a bleed. By now, we had left our suitcases partially packed at all times, so it only took a few minutes to head out of town. We were grateful he could go to OU, but also a little concerned. We had spent so many days at Deaconess, and felt the doctors and nurses knew each and every nuance to care for Benj. OU was a whole different kind of care. We prayed God's plan included those physicians and nurses.

Benji

Over the next ten days or so, I was in the ICU, as well as NPO (no food or water by mouth), because they couldn't find the bleed. They were hoping to find the bleed by doing CT scans and operating as soon as they did find it. If you have food or water, they can't operate, due to the risk of aspiration. At this time, there was blood in my stools and I was occasionally still throwing up some additional blood. I was getting weaker as the days went by, because I was only getting IV fluids and minimal nutrition. My dad finally said something to the head doctor in the ICU about my lack of nutrition, and what were we going to have to do to get me something, because I was losing more weight and getting weaker every single day.

I had never seen a doctor chew out other people in front of a patient like that ICU doctor did. He brought every doctor, resident and med student that was in the area together to ask what was going on. They told him what they were doing to try to find the bleed and they were having some issues getting help from some of the departments. He explained to them how they were doctors, and they gave orders when they wanted things done; they were not to ask about doing something for a patient. He said, "You tell them what you want done for your patient!" He gave three or four of them orders for what he wanted done, right then, and they were jumping to do it! He turned around, nodded, just said to let him know if there were any other issues, and walked away. God Bless that doctor!

November 14th: Today they did an ERCP, removed the drain that went to the common bile duct, and internalized it. Dr. Maple also removed the stent he had in the pseudocyst and installed three new ones. They were keeping me in ICU for a couple of more days then would be moving me to a regular room while, hopefully, they would find the bleed. For some reason, every time they did the CT scan, the bleed never showed up. Multiple doctors had come by, but nobody could come up with a reason for the bleed and why they couldn't find it.

I guess this is as good a time as any to mention that I have been on narcotic pain pills and/or IV pain medication since June; I am clinically dependent on them at this time. It was very difficult for me to understand the difference between dependent and addicted. Basically, dependent means your body requires the medicine to get rid of the pain and be able to function, but there is no high/euphoria like you get if you are addicted.

Pancreatitis is very painful and they have had to continually increase my doses over the past few months to control the pain. I am currently taking oral NORCO and IV Dilaudid, and the pain has only been somewhat controlled.

Now, I want to state that this next part was so difficult to write and it was difficult at the time, but I hold no ill will towards the person I'm going to write about. We all make mistakes; hopefully, we learn from them. The resident on my medical team on November 18th changed my pain medication to oral only. Then he was gone for the weekend and not on call. When a doctor makes a change like this to their patient, the other doctors who are working do not like to override their decision and go back to where that patient's status was. So, they really limited my IV pain meds by only giving them to me every 12 hours, instead of every four, until Monday morning, when the resident came back.

I will say, when he walked into my room on Monday morning, he was not prepared for the wrath he received. I not so politely explained to him how he will never do that to me (or anyone else) again. To any doctors reading this you *never* change meds like this and then leave, especially without informing the patient. I know he learned something on that day and he will think about it with every patient he has, going forward. I completely understand what he was trying to do and I appreciate him doing his best to help get me get off the narcotic pain medication, but this was definitely not the way to do it.

I like to think this single issue will have a lasting effect on many doctors in the future, because his supervisor, Dr. Able from my GI team, was teaching a class the same week and told the story to the students; she explained what had happened (without using names) and she said every single student in the room listened, because she made sure they understood how big an issue it was. I want to say it again: At the time, I was not happy with the situation, but I hold no ill will towards the doctor and hope he learned something about general patient care that day. I am certain he is now a phenomenal doctor, because I can tell you, from that day forward, he explained things to me better than anyone, and I greatly appreciated him doing this.

During this time in the hospital, I started to retain lots of fluid in my abdomen and legs and it was causing quite a bit of pain. Basically, if anyone touched my skin, it was like pushing on a water balloon. Dr. Hancock used an ultrasound to locate the fluid build-up (ascites) in my abdomen and went in with a long needle (this procedure is called paracentesis) and removed almost six liters of fluid. I looked like a completely different person with that much fluid drained from my body.

Dillon

This was also the time I was becoming very concerned he was getting addicted to his pain medication. Working in the emergency department, unfortunately, this is something I see on a daily basis. I heard Benji saying a lot of the same phrases and having the same thoughts I see from those addicted patients. He had been on pain medications for four or five months at this point, with medical conditions that I know will cause severe pain. I know he had worked up quite a tolerance at this point. His pain medication was the one thing he had some control over, meaning he couldn't make himself heal faster, get out of the hospital faster, and persuade the doctors to remove all of the drains he had faster. But he did have some control on when he could ask for more pain medications. I think the depression, anger, malnourishment and having trouble seeing a light at the end of the tunnel when he would be back to himself physically all led to this. Luckily, this didn't last long. They were finally able to remove all the tubes. His GI doctor was able to go in and start cleaning out all the dead pancreatic tissue and Benji was able to get home and start eating and gaining some weight.

Janelle

Tough times. No other words to describe this part of the path to recovery. Both Benji and I could hear the same words from the doctors, but sometimes we would remember different outcomes. I finally received permission to wheel him in the wheelchair down to the cafeteria, where there were windows and sunshine. It was a real struggle, because they didn't want him out of their sight, and there really wasn't a timeframe when doctors might show up to make rounds. But I persisted and I truly think it helped both of us to get out of the hospital room and at least get to see some trees and the outdoors. Looking for better days to come!

Davina

November 18th – Davina's Facebook post: I am so very thankful for so many things. Today I have peace & security in the midst of raging storms. While the winds have slowed, we aren't quite to smooth sailing just yet.

It's the ship's crew that amazes me. We are humbled by the continued outpouring of support during Benji's health challenges. We could not ask for a better support system. We cherish your love and prayers. It is working! Please keep them coming.

Benji

November 19th: Today was opening day of deer gun season in Oklahoma, and I was stuck in the hospital. Again! I don't think I have missed an opening day since I started deer hunting in 1996. It was a tough day for me. I had to wish all my friends good luck.

Benji Evans updated his status. •••

Nov 20, 2016 ·

As pretty much everyone knows it has been a really rough second half of the year for me health wise. I couldn't be more lucky than to have the support that I have had from all of my family but my wife Davina Evans and my parents Brad and Janelle Uhrig Evans Jodi Weyers have just gone above and beyond

There are another group that I would like to thank. As you all know I love to hunt and fish. I have had the chance to deer hunt a couple of times but nothing like I normally do. There are a couple of guys that have offered to do all they could to get me in the woods including driving me right to a blind and carrying any and all of my gear. I am stuck in the hospital this opening weekend of rifle season but may the Bucks stand broadside and may your bullets fly true for the generosity you have shown me. I know that this is not a complete list of the people that have offered to help but it's a start. Spencer Grace Aaron Ghaemi Bryan Robertson and his dad Jim Micheal Blunk and Tadd Tompkins.

 Davina Evans and 123 others   24 Comments 1 Share

November 20th – Benji Facebook post

119

Davina Evans is with **Jodi Evans Weyers** · · ·
and **3 others**.

November 20, 2016 ·

#prayforBenji Calling all prayer warriors! **Benji Evans** is currently in OU Medical Center. He was flown out last Friday vomiting blood. Benji was in hemorrhagic shock & was a bit septic. Thankfully they were able to stabilize him quickly & he is doing well overall. However, they still have not been able to find the source of the bleed. Benji has the leading experts in their field as physicians; I know he is in good hands. Please pray they find & correct the bleed quickly. And I would love if they could do this & get him home for Thanksgiving!

God has already performed many miracles in Benji's life. I know without a doubt God still has plans for Benji & I. Thanks so much for your love & support. Prayer works-especially in large numbers! God is faithful.

😊👍🥰 245   163 Comments 7 Shares

November 20th – Davina Facebook post

Benji

November 24th: Today was Thanksgiving and I somehow talked my medical team into releasing me from the hospital today. I explained how Thanksgiving was my mom's favorite holiday, and I wanted to be able to spend it at home with my wife.

We still hadn't found the bleed, but I was losing less blood each day. I figured I could be more comfortable at home and I'd just go back to the hospital later, if the bleed started up again. Davina brought me home, and shortly after getting there, our good friend Casey Rowe brought us each a full Thanksgiving Day plate. Turkey, dressing, potatoes, gravy... It was a complete meal. Debbie and Dave Schaller also brought over some of her homemade rolls, which are absolutely to die for. I will say it was one of the greatest days I'd had for the past couple of months. I was really weak, but my spirits were on a high just being home on a holiday.

Janelle

My favorite holiday! Everyone will be where they should be today. Benji and Davina are headed home from the hospital, Jeff and Jodi and their kids are in Stephenville, and we are headed home to Cleburne.

Thank you God for ALL of our Blessings!

Davina

November 24th: Wonderful news! Benji was released from the hospital today. He made it home for Thanksgiving after all! We appreciate your prayers more than you know. Prayer truly does work. Love & blessings.

Benji & Davina Evans

***

Bleeding Again

November 25th: It is about 10 pm and I have been home for about 30 hours. I can feel a little bit of fluid under the bandage around my large drain, which is not uncommon, so I ask Davina to get some medical tape and just cover it. I don't want to take the time to redo the bandage before bed. I lay back on the couch as she goes to get the tape, but when I raise my shirt, the bandage is bulging because it is full of blood. I yell to Davina to get an old towel because I am bleeding. She brings it to me and the bandage bursts open from the pressure of the blood. She has to go and get another towel, because I completely filled the first one. I tell her to call an ambulance and she grabs both of our phones. She just stares at both of them. Hers is about out of battery and she can't remember my password. I tell her to put one phone down and call 911.

It took just a few minutes for the ambulance to arrive and our neighbors Mark and Marcy were just getting home as it went by, so they followed it to the house and walked in before the paramedics. When the paramedics walked in, one of them asked if he had been to the house recently. He was the same guy who had taken me to the hospital exactly two weeks before.

They took me back to the Ponca City ER. One funny thing that happened was a chain of phone calls resulting from the dispatch of the ambulance. Christi, an administrative assistant at the bank, heard the call out on the scanner, so she called my assistant Denise, who called another co-worker Dayna, who called her sister-in-law Toni, who was the owner of the pharmacy where Davina worked at the time.

They all showed up at the hospital to see how I was doing. It was starting to look like a work party with everyone showing up. The doctor gave me more blood and called in the helicopter once again, then said I was headed back to OU. One of the cool things was, I received a unit of blood while on the helicopter ride back to OU, and it was from a first-time blood donor!

Janelle

Davina made another CALL to us. We are on our way.

Benji

I do think it is important to say how phenomenal the flight crews were on each of the three flights. They were very professional and caring. They did everything they could to make sure I was comfortable all the time. The only problem I had with the life-flights was, I didn't get frequent flier miles. You would think, after three flights, they would send me a hat or something,

November 26th: I have another CT scan in an attempt to find the bleed, but once again, they can't find it. The doctors are getting frustrated, and you can only imagine how much it is bothering me at this point. I am even beginning to wonder if I should be going to another hospital to see if they can figure something out.

This morning my medical team (hospitalist and the rest of her team) came by and the same doctor who saw me a couple of days before was one of them. She said she had some concerns two days before when I was discharged, that I could end up back in the hospital to find the bleed, but she had hoped it wouldn't be so soon.

Once again, Dr. Hancock went in this week and took another six liters of fluid off my abdomen. This was a total of 12 liters of fluid in two weeks. I had been put on a medication, hopefully to make the fluid in my legs go down, because that had been building up, along with my abdomen. The large drain in my side was also causing lots of pain, and for the past couple of weeks, I had been requesting for it to be removed.

One morning, the surgery team (two doctors) came into my room to explain how the drain was in the exact perfect place to drain fluid from the pseudocyst, and they really would like to leave it where it is. If they did remove it, but at some point, decided I needed it again, they would have to do another surgery to install a new one. They told me I also needed to let the nurses flush it at least twice a day. I explained to them how, when the nurses flushed it, the fluid just came right back out and it was very painful. Reluctantly, I told tell them I would try to leave it in for a couple more days.

It wasn't thirty minutes later when Dr. Able and my GI team (five doctors/students) came in to tell me they were going to remove the drain. I explained to her I was getting ready to say some not so nice things; she said to let her have it.

The only time I felt like I was a *bad* patient (there were times I wasn't great) was during the next 10 minutes or so. I said some very bad things about the communication of my doctors and how, if the doctors taking care of me weren't going to work together to get me taken care of, I would go to another hospital that would. She took my chewing-out like a champ, and nodded her head with everything I said. I told her I wanted Dr. Maple and Dr. Postier in my room, in one of their offices, or in a conference room, or I was going somewhere else that day.

She pulled out her phone, called Dr. Maple from the hallway, and told him what I'd said. Dr. Maple said he would call Dr. Postier and come up with a plan. She came back in about an hour later after talking to Dr. Maple multiple times. She said the drain was coming out. She was going to get me a pain pill now, and she would be back in half an hour to pull the drain. When she came back to pull the drain, she also had Dilaudid; she told me that removing the drain was going to hurt.

I thought there was only about 15 cm of drain inside, because that was the number I could see on the drain hose that was outside my body. When she pulled the drain out, she went hand over hand two or three times. There must have been about two feet inside, and it definitely did hurt coming out. When she got the drain out, there was a blood clot filling up about three or four inches of the bottom of the tube. That was why the drain hadn't been working properly. Everyone was very happy the drain was removed, because it definitely could have been a major problem if the clot had been pushed out of the drain.

Janelle

Frustrating is the only word I can use during this time. Benji is spot on with his description of this particular day. It was so confusing when one doctor said they were going to pull the drain, but then another doctor would come in a few minutes later and say, no, they wouldn't be doing that. All the while, Benji was in pain, with nothing lowering the pain level. Tough day for both of us. Tough day.

Davina

November 27th – Davina's Facebook post: So very true. For me it was a text message on Father's Day morning. Benji & I are very different than we were 6 months ago. We were blissfully happy & unaware of how well life was treating us. Now we are so very thankful & humbled God chose to give us more time together. We continue to be in awe of the love & prayers from our family & friends. We are very different; we are stronger as a couple. We appreciate life's simple pleasures. We are keenly aware of how precious & fragile life is. We are different, but different does not imply we are worse.

> *We are all just a car crash,*
> *a diagnosis, an unexpected phone call,*
> *a newfound love, or a broken heart*
> *away from becoming a completely*
> *different person.*
> *How beautifully fragile are we*
> *that so many things can take but a moment*
> *to alter who we are*
> *for forever?*[1]

---

[1] S. D. Thompson. (n.d). *Fragile*. Retrieved from https://allpoetry.com/poem/12202196-Fragile-by-Sam-D.-Thompson

Benji

December 1st: To say I am ready to get back home is an understatement. Today, my medical team came in and said I have an infection in my blood. It is some type of fungus (I don't have any clue how to say or spell it). They are fairly concerned about it, but have agreed to go ahead and send me home with intravenous IV antibiotics. They put in a PICC Line to allow us to do everything at home. They will show Davina how to give me the antibiotics; I am not able to attach the antibiotic bottle to the IV because of where it is in my arm.

They allowed me to go home on Saturday the 2nd. On Sunday, Davina was able to put the Christmas tree up to try and make it a somewhat normal December for us

December 4th: My parents are up once again and are cooking lots of soups and stews for us. They wanted to do something that would be easy for me to heat up when Davina was at work. Today is also the last day of the Oklahoma deer gun season. Having spent almost every day since November 19th in the hospital, I have not been able to go hunting since mid-October. Spencer called and is going to take me out tonight. He has an enclosed blind I can sit in and I won't be cold.

He was even able to drive me right up to it. There were about 10 stairs walking up to the blind. I carried some of my gear up, and it absolutely wore me out. I was down to about 130 pounds and really didn't have any strength at all. We sat there for a couple of hours and saw some deer at the other end of the field. They were too far away to shoot, which wouldn't be an issue on a normal day, because we would just get down and go after them. Today, there was no way I would've been able to get down to chase them.

It was a beautiful day and I was so grateful to spend an afternoon in the woods with a great friend. This was the fifth hunt of the season for me. I will remember those five hunts the rest of my life, even though an animal wasn't harvested. For those of you who are hunters, you understand what I am saying.

Benji and Spencer heading to the woods for the last deer hunt of the season. This was about as bad as Benji ever looked. He weighed around 130 pounds, down from 195.

Davina

December 5th – Davina's Facebook post: #pray-forBenji. Benji Evans & I had a wonderful weekend. He made it home late Saturday afternoon. We celebrated with a very nice steak dinner with Brad & Janelle Uhrig Evans & even managed a add a little holiday cheer! We cherish all your prayers.

Benji

December 6th: The doctors at Deaconess Hospital had told us there would be setbacks throughout this process, but we didn't have any clue how many and how bad they were going to be. I feel like we just can't catch a break. Today, I was going to see Dr. O'Neal in Ponca City (he came to Ponca City one day a month) since he was the doctor in charge, when I was going to be released to go back to work. I hadn't been to see him since the bleeding began.

I stopped at the bathroom in his building on the way to see him, and looked down and saw blood on the floor. I opened up my jacket and the left side of my shirt was covered in blood. I lifted my shirt up and blood was pouring out of the hole where the large drain (which had just been removed) had been located. I grabbed a bunch of paper towels to try to control the blood flow and called his office to tell them what was happening.

Of course, they said to go to the ER so I just walked across the parking lot. When I walked into the ER, there was a patient at the check-in window. I didn't want to wait, so I walked right up and said I had a severe bleed in my abdomen and needed to be seen immediately. The receptionist yelled at another person who came around and asked if I was a knife wound victim. I told her it was from where a drain had just been removed. When she saw the blood, she rushed me into a room, I explained what had been happening, and they took me in for a CT scan. To make matters worse, I started throwing up blood again. I had an appointment with Dr. Maple the next day for another debridement, so I called; they said to plan on coming for the appointment but wanted me to bring the CT with me.

As if we hadn't had enough bad news the past six months, this afternoon Davina got a call from her sister saying their dad was being transported to Baptist Hospital in Oklahoma City because he had suffered another stroke.

The original plan was for me to have a former co-worker, Dave Schaller, take me down for the procedure at around 5:00 am the next day, but we decided to go ahead and head down tonight, so Davina could go and be with her dad. Due to the infections I had, we decided it would be best if I just stayed in the hotel while she went to see him. I crashed as soon as we got there, because there is nothing more tiring than being in an ER room for half the day.

Dillon

Unfortunately, Benji had several episodes when he started having severe bleeding from and around the tube draining the pseudocyst. He required multiple admissions for this, as well as multiple blood transfusions. He was in the hospital for days on end, without much really happening. They couldn't figure out where the bleeding was coming from for quite some time, and it seemed to him he was just sitting there waiting to see if he was going to continue to bleed. They were finally able to find the area of bleeding and they were able to get it stopped.

Then, there were several long admissions, because they couldn't decide about the possibility of removing the tube draining the pseudocyst. I bring this up because this is one time, I saw it really affecting Benji mentally and emotionally.

He became depressed and angry. I totally understand these feelings. I know I would have had them long before he did. At this point, he had mainly been living in the hospital for six months. He was extremely malnourished, to the point his abdomen was distended and he had severe swelling of his legs.

When you become that malnourished, the body does not have building blocks to make proteins in the blood to help hold onto fluid in the blood vessels. Because of this, fluid leaks out of the vessels and into the abdomen, lungs and extremities. They were draining this fluid off so he was more comfortable, but he just didn't have any appetite. This was obviously related to him being so sick for so long, and being in the hospital for so long, where the food really sucked. Looking back, I think he was becoming depressed because he wasn't getting better.

I remember coming around a corner at work and seeing Davina standing in the hallway right outside of one of the ER rooms. I was shocked to see her standing there, and wondered what had happened. That's when she told me she was there with her dad and they thought he'd just had another stoke. I went in to say hi to them, and to let me know, if they needed anything, to let me know, as one of my partners was the physician taking care of them. I just remember walking out of that room with the feeling of "How can this family – not catch a break?"

Benji

December 7th: Dr. Maple went in to do the debridement of the pseudocyst this morning, but the food I had eaten the night before hadn't digested in my stomach, so he wasn't able to get anything done. Don't ever eat beef jerky the night before a surgery. There was some mild concern doing this procedure, due to the blood loss from the previous 24 hours, but there were not any complications.

This afternoon, Dr. Hancock went in again and removed 3.3 liters of fluid off my abdomen. They also reviewed the CT scan while I was having the procedure done.

They finally found the bleed! I have an aneurysm on the splenic artery, which supplies blood to the spleen.

The interventional radiology team decided they were going to put a coil in my splenic artery by going up through my femoral artery. The biggest concern with this was that the artery could close up and cause a major bleed. The other issue was that this coil could possibly cut off the blood flow to my spleen and cause it to die. They were able to do the procedure. While they were in there, they found two more aneurysms, so they installed two coils. This concerned me some, because I knew there was a greater chance of losing my spleen now.

December 21st: I went in today for another paracentesis procedure by Dr. Hancock. This is the fourth and final time they are going to do this procedure, and they pulled out another 3.4 liters. They pulled out a total of almost 19 liters. Each time they removed the fluid, my pain level has gone down and I generally just felt better. It was a simple procedure (for me at least) and was worth doing each time.

***

Christmas Is Coming

Benji

December 24th: My parents, sister (Jodi), brother-in-law (Jeff), niece (Reese) and nephew (Mason) have come up to celebrate Christmas with Davina and me. It is such a great feeling to be home for the holidays and be able to see everyone. Except...

Tonight, I started to cramp up again. It wasn't nearly as severe as the last time, so I drank some PowerAde and water and made it through the night. On Christmas morning, I was having lots of pain, was very weak, and really couldn't get out of my recliner; I told everyone to go ahead and open their presents. I didn't make it all the way through the present opening; I started throwing up.

I felt horrible for Reese and Mason to have seen me like this. Once again, Davina took me to the ER. We were there for most of the day. They gave me more Dilaudid to get the pain under control and did another CT scan, just to see if anything new had popped up. I finally made it home late in the afternoon, and was able to just relax and enjoy being with family. By the next day, I was feeling much better.

Davina

December 25th – Davina Facebook post: Benji gifted me with the only thing I could ask for from him this year-the gift of time. Time to grow old together. And yes, it was actually a gift only God could give. Benji defied all the odds after coding 3 times after a life-threatening case of pancreatitis. Our life hasn't been the same since but we still have each other. Benji & I share the same primary love language-quality time. Cheers to having many more years together! Love you mean it Benji. Thanks for loving me so well.

Janelle

It's Christmas Day and we are all together in Ponca City. Jeff, Jodi and the kids are here and we opened part of our presents, but Benji was in horrible pain; Davina and he spent part of the day in the ER so he could get IV fluids. When they got home, we had a nice meal and opened the rest of our presents. It wasn't a normal Christmas Day, it wasn't even a semi-normal Christmas Day, but we were all together and I've learned this is all that really matters. I am trying to be grateful and thankful.

Chapter 8

A New Year Begins

Benji
January 9th, 2017:

January 9th, 2017: I was scheduled to have another debridement on the 23rd, but because I've been running a fairly high fever the past few days, they moved the procedure to today. This is the longest I have gone without some type of procedure since September.

When I woke up after the procedure, Dr. Maple said he had gotten everything. This was something we have been waiting to hear for the past six months! He wants me to do another CT scan in 30 days, just to make sure everything looks good. He doesn't know why I am having the fever at this time. To be honest, it is at the back of my mind, since we have the best news we have had since this all started.

Janelle

I couldn't be smiling any bigger than I am today. On the road to recovery!

So grateful and thankful. Thank you, God, for Your healing miracles!

Benji

January 11th: Today I went to meet my new endocrinologist, Dr. Kipgen, in Stillwater. She just can't believe, with everything that has happened to me, that I am still alive. I told her the same thing everyone said when I woke from the coma, "God has a plan for me."

I weigh 132 pounds at this time, which is down over 60 pounds from where I started. Dr. Kipgen wants me to come back next week to meet with a nutritionist to find a way to increase my calorie intake (I can't eat a very big meal at this time) to try to get some weight back on me. Now that I basically don't have a pancreas, I am 100% reliant on insulin. Dr. Kipgen did a fantastic job of explaining to me how my life will be different, going forward. In the hospital system, they give you enough insulin to keep you alive. Dr. Kipgen helped me understand how I would be using insulin so I can live a fairly normal life.

The number of times she has replied to my emails since that first meeting after 5:00 pm is mind-blowing to me. I couldn't ask for a better Endo. Thank you, Dr. Kipgen and your nurse Amber who just loves to torment me!

January 31st: Back in December, between hospital stays, I met at the bank with my boss, Jeff and Kelli, the HR Director. The decision was made that if I wasn't able to come back to work full time by January 31st, they would have to let me go; they need to fill my position. I completely understand this. There is no way I will be able to get back to work in the near future. It wasn't easy, but I cleaned out my office and told everyone I would be back once I was feeling better.

***

Texas Blood Drive

Benji

February 16th: Jodi and Jeff own a coffee shop and hot dog restaurant called Beans and Franks in Stephenville, Texas. Our family now knows how important it is to give blood, since I received so much during my illness, so Jodi called the blood drive coordinator for her area, told them my story, and said she wanted to do a blood drive based at the restaurant.

The blood bank was happy to have a new place to do a blood drive, and said they would put something in the local newspaper, but Jodi said she would take care of the ad. Jodi is good friends with Sara, the editor of the paper, so she called her, told her what she was planning, and asked if she could purchase a small ad in the paper. Sara told her, instead of an ad in the paper, she would like to write a front-page article about the need for blood and to tell my story.

They did a three-and-a-half-hour blood drive and had to turn people away. We have seen, firsthand, when there is a story to go with a need, it touches so many more people and they are willing to give more often.

***

Continued Blessings

Benji

I don't know the exact date, but sometime in February I had a tooth that was very painful. A friend of mine, Cristy, worked at a dental office and was always calling to check on me and see if there was anything she could do. I called her and explained what was happening, and she got me right in. They took x-rays of my teeth and couldn't find anything. I didn't have dental insurance at the time, so I was just happy I wasn't going to get a bunch of work done. The dentist, Dr. Buchanan, came in and said to come back if I had any problems; he added that Cristy had told him everything I had been through, and he wasn't going to charge me anything. I tried to explain how I was happy to pay, but he wouldn't take anything.

He was another person doing something nice for me during my illness. I now consider him a friend, and I have been blessed to share the deer woods with him on two occasions when he harvested his first two deer. Taking him hunting was the least I could do, after he was willing to help me when I needed it.

February 28th: Prince of Peace Lutheran Church hosts a Fat Tuesday Pancake Supper fundraiser each year to support either an organization or family in the community. They called and asked if we would be willing to be a recipient this year. When they first called, I said there were many more deserving people than us, and I didn't think we could accept the funds. I told Davina about it that night, and we decided we would be willing to do half, if they could split it with another family who had been through something terrible over the past year. They said the fundraiser is for one person/family, so we decided to accept their offer of help.

I was able to spend about two hours at the door, thanking people for their donations. There were lots of people I knew, who wanted to come by to show their support, but there were also so many I didn't know. I will never forget one family that came in. There were two adults and six kids, so their "bill" should have been $30, but they paid with a $100 bill and said to keep the change. I had never met these people before and they were willing to give money to help a family to which they had no ties. I don't know who they are, but I hope they know how touching this was to me.

When the church delivered the check to us the next week, they said there had been the most people they had ever served, and the most money they had ever raised. The Ponca City community did so many things for us, and wanted nothing in return. We will forever be grateful for all the acts of kindness shown to us.

From left to right - Roberta Shaffer, Bev and Chuck Schneider and Ray Shaffer with Benji at the Pancake Supper. Chuck did so much for Benji and Davina during his illness.

Allen and Bev Taylor with Benji at the Pancake Supper

***

Love Those Nurses

Benji

March 8th: Jodi told the nurses in the CCU how I loved to cook barbecue for people. She kept telling them that *when* I got healthy, I would cook for them. I was able to get in touch with Meg, who was off that day but was willing to meet me at the hospital. She also brought her husband and son for me to meet. I was able to feed dinner to the day nurses and lunch to the overnight nurses; we served smoked chicken and Davina made lemon cupcakes. It was so nice to be able to thank those nurses in person for being such a huge part of saving my life.

Most of them didn't recognize me because I had lost so much weight, but once I said that I was in Room "89" with the high triglycerides, they knew exactly who I was. Jodi posted a picture of Meg and me on Facebook from that day, and some of the nurses were trying to figure out how they didn't know me. When we told them what had been wrong with me, they knew exactly who I was. Then they said something along the lines of, "I took care of you one night." "I loved your wife and parents." "They really took over the waiting room." "You sure look different than the last time I saw you."

Some of the nurses (angels) from Deaconess. Nurse Jeff is second from the left.

***

First Trip

March 15th: My nephew Mason had a baseball tournament in Waco, so I decided to go and spend a couple of days with the family in Texas. My parents and I met Jodi and her family for the games and I really enjoyed seeing the boys play ball and visit with the parents of the kids. All weekend, I heard, "We have been praying for you." It was great to meet more of the prayer warriors I had on my side.

While in Texas, we also were able to go out to the Burseys' house for an afternoon. They have a pond with lots of largemouth bass. I still wasn't strong enough to stand and fish for hours, but I was able to sit in a chair and move it around as needed and catch a few fish. Reese put it on all of us and caught the most, but we all had a great time. It was a phenomenal time to get to do something "normal."

Dad also brought out his rifle because he wasn't sure it was sighted in. I shot it about five times to make sure it was sighted in and that was all I could handle. The punch was just too much with all the weight I had lost.

Mason showing his Uncle Benji how to catch fish!!!

New Addition

April 5th: I decided I needed a new hunting dog I could train with all of my down time and I am feeling better each and every day. So, Davina and I picked out a Golden Retriever and I brought him home today. Ruger was born on Valentine's Day. He took up much more energy than I expected over the coming months. At this point, I had the time on my hands to work with him, but to do so with energy was a completely different thing. It was great having a puppy around, but I am not sure our other four dogs felt the same way. His endless energy was a drain on me, but it also brought a smile to my face. Other than chewing on anything he could find in the kitchen, the underground electric fence, firewood in the back yard, and anything else he could get his mouth on, he was a great partner for me.

Sadly, he got out the next January and was hit by a car. Ruger, we didn't have you for long, but you were a huge part of my healing process.

Turkey Hunt

April 7th: I have decided to go out to hunt turkeys in Western Oklahoma, where my best friend Tyke lives with his wife Mandy and their twins Brandt and Launa. When I hunted last fall, it was all about just going out and spending time in the woods. I will say, this trip was all about harvesting a turkey or two.

My good friend Micheal decided to go with me on the long drive out there, which was a blessing, because I wasn't sure how my body would handle it. He had come down to see me every weekend when I was in the coma, so it was nice to have a chance to take him on a hunt and thank him for being there for me.

We got there on Friday night and almost immediately heard turkeys gobbling, so we decided to get dressed and try to get a bird. When we told the twins we were going turkey hunting, Launa got out with her little folding chair and sat in the driveway. The turkeys come right through their yard, so she thought we were going to shoot them right there. It was one of the funniest things I have ever seen.

Michael and I went into the woods, called up a bird to about 15 yards, and I was able to harvest it. It was the first time as an adult I have ever had tears coming down my face from shooting an animal. Michael just had some "allergies" bothering his eyes at the moment. Standing over the bird I had harvested was kind of a turning point for me. At the time, I knew I was getting back to being me. It was all about being with great friends and doing what I love. The next morning, Michael and I each got another turkey. It was definitely in the Top Five hunts of my life.

Benji Evans added 2 new photos.
April 8, 2017 · 🌐   ...

9 months ago these two guys weren't sure that I was ever going to get to hunt with them again (or survive at all). Yesterday and today I got to turkey with two of my best friends. **Tyke Greer** has been my best friend since the nursery at church. **Micheal Blunk** has taught me pretty much everything I know about turkey hunting and a ton about hunting in general. I can't thank you guys enough for hunting with me this weekend. It meant the world to me

👍 Write a comment...   👍 Write a comment...

👍❤️😮 244   22 Comments 4 Shares

April 8th - Benji's Facebook post

144

Benji

April 10th: Justin Sober had told me where to hunt for turkeys on his place, so I went out late this morning to see if I could get my third and final bird for the year. I was able to call up a large tom and harvest it with my Grandad's old 16-gauge shotgun. After firing that shot, the emotions just came crashing down on me. I sat there on the ground and cried like a baby. My first hunt, out on my own, getting to harvest an animal after being so sick, plus getting it with my grandad's gun... filled me beyond full. Besides, that was my first time ever to fill out the limit on turkeys....

All of this, and even I, finally felt like it was the beginning of the end of my illness.

Janelle

We had the *best* phone call from Benji; he sounded like he felt so good today! The story he told us brought tears to our eyes. His grandad would have been so proud of him, and of his bravery this past year!

We are Grateful and Thankful.

Benji

May 5th: Today, with Davina beside me, I had an appointment with Dr. Maple to discuss the plans going forward. I have been on insulin for months now. This has been because, in my mind, my pancreas just wasn't working. I asked Dr. Maple about undergoing a surgery called a pancreatic islet transplant, which a doctor friend in Texas had told me about.

Basically, they take cells from your pancreas, insert them into your liver, and it will then produce insulin for your body. Dr. Maple's answer was, "That ship has sailed. Your pancreas exploded."

That punched me like a sledgehammer! I guess it explained all of the debridement procedures I had to have done. Dr. Maple had been pulling out the pieces of my pancreas and they were just like strings. That's how I found out I had very little of the head and tail of my pancreas left.

Chapter 9

New Mission – Ambassador

With all the blood donated in my name, I received a letter from Oklahoma Blood Institute (OBI) saying I could get a reimbursement for some of the costs of the blood I had received. Before it was all said and done, I had received 42 units of blood, one of plasma, and one of platelets, so my costs were fairly high.

When I called to get more information, I talked to a woman named Shelly, and after talking with her for a while, I said they could spend the money better than I could, and help save another life; I said they could just keep those funds.

Shelly asked me if I was willing to tell her the reason, I had needed so much blood. After telling her my story, she asked if I would be willing to be an OBI Ambassador and come down to speak to the employees at the contact center.

How could I say no to people who had been such a big part of saving my life?

Davina and I stopped on the way home from seeing Dr. Maple on May 5th, and gave our story to about 60 call center employees and 40 managers from across the region that OBI serves. This was my first speech. There were lots of tears flowing, and most of them from me! It was such a great feeling to thank the people who ask others to give blood. There is no doubt in my mind; some of the blood I received came from a phone call one of the people in that room made to a donor to ask them to donate.

Father's Day 2017

June 17th: We are having a Father's Day dinner at Davina's sister Liz's house; it's a day early to celebrate my gift of life one year later, and another Father's Day with her dad, after his strokes. I had called my parents to ask them if they would be able to come up and celebrate with us. Dad said there was just no way for them to be able to make it, which I completely understood because it was a four-hour drive.

We arrived and had the chance to say hi to her parents, Glen and Josy, as well as her other sister Becky, her husband Curtis, and our nephews, William and Jerram. Then, out of the bedroom walk my parents, along with Dad's cousin Gary and his wife Loretta.

To say it was a surprise is an understatement! I am good at pulling those kinds of pranks on other people, but they weren't supposed to do it to me.

It was great to celebrate the year with our families. It had been such a difficult year for all of us, but we made it through, and are very grateful for the time with the ones we love. This was a special Father's Day, not only because I was able to spend it with my father, but this was also the last Father's Day Davina got to spend with hers. We lost Glen to leukemia in November.

June 18th – Brad and Benji on Father's Day 2017 exactly one year after he went to the hospital. The Evans family always has plenty of food to cook and Benji cooked all of this for the lunch.

June 18th, Benji's Facebook post: What's in a year? When you are 15 and waiting to get your driver's license, that year takes forever. When you are 29, it rushes into 30 almost overnight. When you are on death's doorstep at any age the days pass so slowly at times you can't stand it. At other times it flies right by. Today marks the one-year anniversary of me getting sick and knocking on that door more times than I want to remember. Difficult doesn't even touch what this year has been like for us. I spent over 100 days in the hospital, 3 life flights, an ambulance ride and many trips by car to the hospital. It is not something that I expected to happen when I was 35-36. It was a trial to test my faith but was also a way to see the love from so many people. Today is the first anniversary of my "new life". The struggles will continue but I know that with friends and family we will continue to persevere. I will never be able to thank everyone that came to the hospital to see me. But what I appreciate more than that is the support that you gave to my family in those darkest of hours. For that I am eternally grateful.

Yesterday was a great day. My parents, Brad and Janelle, and my cousins, Gary and Loretta Harding, showed up in Edmond to celebrate the Father's Day we were having with Davina's family. Thank you to the whole Sill family for the surprise, and for letting me spend some time with my family when we had planned to just spend it with you.

Jodi Weyers, I thought we had each other's back and I promise I will get you for not letting me in on the secret!

Janelle

To say it was the best day ever is an understatement! Oh, how we loved celebrating the day of life with you and Davina, and yes, it was *so* great surprising the two of you! We are grateful and thankful beyond words!

150

Brutus

Benji

When they made the first incision back in June 2016, they left it open for eight days. Then they closed it up and I had the wound-vac machine to pull out any additional fluid. This is also where the fluid was leaking when I had the ascites. At the top of that incision, there was an area where the muscles didn't heal properly; I had an incisional hernia that I lovingly named "Brutus." To be honest, I was waiting for an alien to pop out of it like on *Space-Balls*© (You need to watch this video if you haven't seen it) Brutus was larger than a softball. He stuck out about five inches when I was sitting or standing. If I lay my stomach, Brutus was flat.

At this time, I weigh about 150 pounds, so I have added back 30 pounds from my lowest weight; I feel like I can handle a full surgery now. I contacted Dr. Postier to get a recommendation on the surgeon I should use for the hernia repair, and he said to use Dr. Raines at OU Medical Center. I scheduled an appointment to meet with him June 21st.

When he walked into the room, I got off the table, shook his hand, and introduced myself. He examined the hernia and told me he had read my file and was really surprised by how I was feeling. He said most patients, when they come in with pancreatitis, not to mention my complications, were usually not in the best of spirits. He couldn't believe I had a positive attitude, and thought it was hilarious I had named my hernia. We scheduled surgery for July 6th.

Vacation

June 24th: After we asked about it, and talked with Dr. Maple in May, he said Davina and I could take a vacation, but he didn't want us to leave the country or have any connecting flights. Some friends of ours offered to let us stay at their place at Table Rock Lake near Branson, Missouri. We decided to drive there today, spend the night, then head up to St. Louis to watch a Cardinals' baseball game. I am so fortunate to have a wife who enjoys baseball almost as much as I do. After a couple of days in St. Louis, we spent the rest of the week at the lake and really enjoyed relaxing together for the first time in a year.

Picture of Benji and Davina at Top of the Rock in Branson, MO just prior to his final surgery

Chapter 10

Final Surgery

July 6th:

July 6th: My parents came up from Texas to bring me down to OUMC for my final surgery. I had told Davina she should just work on Thursday, then come down after work on Friday. Our neighbor Chuck happened to be at the hospital for an outpatient procedure for his mom; he was at the desk, asking if he could go to my room. Dr. Raines happened to be there at the same time and said he was headed to my room, so he brought Chuck down.

They walked into my room together and Dr. Raines said, "I'd like to introduce your surgeon, Chuck." Besides having a great sense of humor, Dr. Raines was a great guy, for sure.

Dr. Raines fixed the hernia and said he thought I would be able to go home the next day. When I woke up from the anesthesia, they told me I had a pain pump and to push the button when I had pain. I apparently didn't remember them telling me it only worked every 20 minutes, because I received about 40 doses and hit the button over 130 times that night. This surgery was more painful than anything else I have had done over the past year.

When Dr. Raines came in Friday morning, he had a big smile on his face. When he saw the usage on the pain pump though, his smile disappeared. He told me he wouldn't let me go home until I was off the pain pump for 24 hours. I agreed there was no way I was going home with the pain I was having. On Saturday, I told them to take the pump away so I could go home on Sunday the 9th.

July 12th: I have been running a fever for a couple of days, so we called Dr. Raines' office and they said he wanted to see me. Davina was so concerned, so she took off from work and went with me. She hadn't met Dr. Raines yet. When he walked into the room, he looked at me and then at Davina, and said for me to hold on because he hadn't met my wife and he wanted to talk to her. He cares about the family just like he cares about the patient; to me, that makes him a really great person as well as a phenomenal surgeon.

They had checked my blood pressure, temperature and heart rate; he said my heart rate was high, but everything else was good. He really just wanted to see me in person and said we could go home, but if the fever wasn't gone by Friday he was going to "put my butt back in the hospital and run a bunch of tests I wasn't going to like." I really appreciated him not admitting me that day, and luckily the fever went away and didn't come back.

July 17th: I had my scheduled follow-up appointment with Dr. Raines today. He was really happy with how the incision was healing. He had basically cut out three inches of scar tissue and pulled the skin together. The new scar was less than a half inch wide and looked much better. At that appointment, he told me, "You make me a better doctor." This was not something I had ever heard before, so I asked what he was talking about. He said with everything I had been through, I had every single right to complain, but he had yet to see me say anything negative. I laughed and said he had only seen me on my good days, because there had definitely been days when I did complain.

He then told me, "The last couple of weeks, I have had things that just didn't go quite right and I got upset about it. Then I thought of you, and everything you have gone through, and know I have nothing to complain about."

I had never thought that everything I had been through, and the way I had reacted and acted, could have had that kind of effect on others. But his saying those words surely showed me how I could have the ability to make an impact on others, and it is my choice to make it a positive or negative. Being positive to this point was just for me; going forward, I decided to do my best to be positive to everyone from now on.

Dillon

It was still several months and probably about one full year since Benji first got sick before I would say he was almost fully recovered. I am still not sure he will ever be truly and fully recovered. He will always have to pay much closer attention to his health and diabetes. But, to see how he made it through, emotionally and spiritually, is truly amazing. I think he would tell you he is blessed to be where he is, which is true. Because for him to still be with us is a miracle.

***
Thanks And Giving Banquet

Benji

August 8th: I received an email today from Sundee, with the Oklahoma Blood Institute. She wasn't able to hear my first speech at OBI, but she had heard about it and had been told I was willing to share my story to show the need for blood and help recruit donors. On September 29th, OBI was going to have a banquet where they bring together blood drive co-ordinators and donors from across the state. They wanted to have a couple of people tell their stories to thank those people involved in putting on blood drives, as well as people who have donated blood. I told her I would be more than happy to tell my story, especially after she told me I might have the opportunity to meet some of my own blood donors.

August 24th: One of the things OBI wanted to do during the banquet was to have a short video of my story. A large part of the video was OBI showing how they supply every helicopter in Oklahoma with O-negative blood. Of course, since I received one of those units, I was more than happy to do the video. Their plan was to play the video to the people in attendance at the banquet and then put it online for people to see. Once again, I shed a couple of tears while telling my story, but there were fewer than when I gave my first speech to OBI.

September 29th: Before the banquet, my family and I were shown into a meeting room with some other people, and I had the chance to meet two of my donors. I have never given a sincerer hug to people I just met than I did to David and Lisa, both of whom had been my donors. It was also great to hug Dr. O'Neal, who was also able to attend with his wife. It was a great surprise to see him there because he didn't RSVP until the day of the event. I also had the opportunity to meet a pilot, a paramedic, and two nurses who had been part of the crews that had flown me from Ponca City to OU Medical Center. It was so good to see them when I wasn't strapped to a gurney. When the banquet started, they played the video showing how all the helicopters in Oklahoma were now supplied with O negative blood from OBI. After the video, I went onstage and invited my donors, Dr. O'Neal, and all the helicopter crews who were in attendance up there with me.

OBI had asked me to say something during this time of dead air, as people were walking up, so I decided to open my speech saying, "You want to talk about a special ten days. My dad's birthday was the 19th, Davina and I had our 4th wedding anniversary on the 20th, Davina's birthday was the 28th, and my birthday is today. This is the biggest birthday party I have ever had! Besides getting to say all that, I got to speak to over 400 people and tell my story of how blood saved my life. I can't imagine a better week and a half." Somehow, I gave the rest of my speech without shedding a tear, but there were lots of wet eyes when I looked across the crowd.

Since August, when they asked me to give the speech, I had been thinking about what verse from the Bible I wanted to use at the end. I would open up my Bible app on my phone and look, but I just couldn't find what I really needed to say. Five days before my speech, our pastor, Rick Hughes, gave a sermon at church and I finally had my ending. He read from the Book of Matthew, Chapter 22:37-38.

Jesus is talking about the two great commandments and says:

"Thou shalt love the Lord thy God with all thy heart, and with all thy soul, and with all thy mind. This is the first and great commandment."

I decided the Second Commandment was the ending to my speech. In Verses 39-40, Jesus says:

"...and the second is like unto it, Thou shalt love thy neighbour as thyself."

I can't think of a single thing a person can do to love another person more than to give them the gift of life. Each of those people on the stage with me had a part in saving my life, especially the five people who gave blood, as well as all the other donors who were not able to attend.

Another blood recipient named John was also a speaker that night. He spoke for just a couple of minutes, then his family spoke about how grateful they were to still have their husband, father, and grandpa there. At the end of the banquet, they called me back up to the stage and brought out a three-tiered Oklahoma State cake and the audience sang Happy Birthday to me. It was definitely the largest birthday party I have ever had!

After the banquet ended, Dr. O'Neal came up to me and explained that he hadn't had any idea about everything I had been through. I hadn't seen him since November 2016, so he didn't know everything about the bleed and the other issues I'd had. I told him I would be happy to sit down with him sometime and tell him about all the complications.

I have no doubt Dr. O'Neal is the doctor who kept me alive long enough to have a fighting chance, and I would do anything for him, especially if it might help save another life.

I also had the opportunity to talk to three more of my donors after the banquet. I will always remember James, Susan, Monty, David, and Lisa. The one thing I did to make sure they didn't forget me was sending each of them men a money clip, and each of the women a key chain with: "I GAVE, HE LIVED" engraved on them. They all said they didn't want anything from me, but I told them I had already purchased something for them so they might as well give me their addresses. These "normal, average" people saved my life by giving blood.

Not all of us can be nurses or doctors, but we can help save a life by donating blood. My one request, if you have read this far in the book, is to go and give the gift of life. You just never know when you might help someone you know.

As James was writing down his address for me, his 10-year-old daughter RJ was just standing there, so I asked her if she understood what tonight had been about. She said she kind of understood it. I explained how we all have more blood than we really need at any one time, and sometimes, people donate a portion of their blood so it can be given to others who need it. Then our body makes new blood, so we are still healthy. I told her how her daddy gave me his blood, and how I received his, as well as blood from many others; now her daddy would be a part of me forever. It all really clicked for her. She kind of puffed out her checks and looked up at her daddy like he was Superman! I can almost guarantee she will be a lifetime blood donor, once she's old enough to donate. At her young age, she had the chance to see, firsthand, the benefit of blood donation.

I was so fortunate to have some of my family and closest friends attend the banquet. Of course, Davina was with me, along with my parents, Davina's sister Liz, Marolyn my neighbor when I was growing up, Gary and Loretta, Fed and Jenelle, Drew and Constance, Tim McCarthey, Dave and Debbie Schaller, and Jeff and Dede Lee. All of them did so much for me during my illness. I was so blessed to have them there to support me.

We also had the opportunity to sit in the lobby with all the family and friends who came to the banquet. It was great having everyone sitting around and talking like we had done many times, but not having to worry about my illness. It felt normal. Once all the family and friends left, Davina and I sat with a couple of the people from the helicopter flight crews and told them my entire story. Speaking with them was a great thing for me, because they had such a huge part in getting me to the hospitals quickly and safely.

Janelle

Oh, what a night it has been! Benji and Davina look so happy, and it is wonderful to see the love they have for each other on this special night. Even though we all shed tears when Benji told his story, there is much laughter and happiness. He is alive because of these donors and First Responders.

We are in awe of God's grace and mercy, and we

are grateful and thankful!!

Benji speaking at the Oklahoma Blood Institute "Thanks and Giving" banquet on September 29th, 2017. This was his 37th birthday where he was able to meet 5 of his blood donors.

From Left to right – *Marolyn, Davina, Benji, Janelle, and Brad at the OBI "Thanks and Giving" banquet.*

From Left to Right - *Constance, Drew, Davina, Benji, Ryan and Jenelle at the OBI "Thanks and Giving" banquet.*

Loretta and Gary drove all the way from Houston to Oklahoma City to attend the OBI "Thanks and Giving" banquet.

Benji and Dr. O'Neal at the OBI "Thanks and Giving" banquet.

Benji getting to meet his blood donor David at the OBI "Thanks and Giving" banquet.

Benji and Davina with his blood donor Lisa.

Benji speaking at the OBI "Thanks and Giving" banquet. **From Left to Right** – *executive and four members of the Air-Evac flight crews, blood donors Lisa, David and Susan, Dr. O'Neal, blood donor Monty, Air-Evac executive, and blood donor James.*

Benji with some of the Air-Evac Crew.

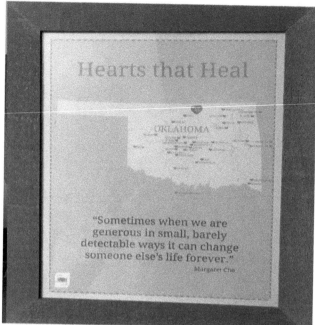

This map shows where all 42 blood donors donated the blood Benji received. Without these people donating, he definitely would not be alive today.

Chapter 11

Re-Cap

To recap everything that happened is an enormous task, but I had 15 surgeries and procedures over a six-month period; I "coded" three times, had three life flights, lost over 70 pounds in six months, and received 42 units of blood. My 16th surgery was 13 months after I first got sick.

Opening Day - Twice

September 2nd:

It is the second day of dove season, but close enough. I saw where the Taylor family had gone hunting yesterday, so I called Ken to see if they were going the next day. He said they were, so I decided to surprise the rest of the crew. I had the chance to sit next to a hay bale with Todd and Evan and shoot a couple of birds. It was great to be back outside wasting a couple shotgun shells.

Todd and Benji on a dove hunt September 2nd, 2017

October 1st:

Today is opening day of deer archery season in Oklahoma. It is kind of a big day for those of us who bow hunt. As hunters, we usually have to take off work to go out on opening day, but I am still not working, so I am able to just go. I know Davina was a nervous wreck when I left the house this morning, but it was something I just had to do. It was good for the mind, heart and soul.

There are many people who believe hunting is

170

about killing animals. To be honest, for a majority of hunters, that is just a small part of the hunt. Hearing the birds wake up with the dawn of a new day; watching the squirrels chase each other up a tree; watching the deer that are out of range and not caring one bit that you won't get a shot at them; all of those moments are the life of an outdoorsman. When you get to spend those days afield, with friends or family like I did last year when I was sick, life just doesn't get much better.

I have had some of my deepest thoughts and most sincere prayers while sitting in a deer stand. Today was another one of those days. I was able to thank God for another day to see the beauty of nature. Today was another day to enjoy the gift of life.

It does not get any better than this!

Benji's Facebook post:

Today is the day. Opening day of deer season. Not sure if I was home or in the hospital a year ago but today, I am in a tree stand doing one of my favorite things in the world. I am so blessed to have the opportunity to be out here and it wouldn't have happened without the care of MANY nurses, doctors, friends and family. The care, calls, thoughts and especially prayers are the only reason I am here today. Thank you all for being there with me

May the wind always be in your face and your shot always be true. Remember it is our love of the outdoors and not the kill that brought us to the woods. Continue the tradition and be safe out there.

P.S. May big bucks come by your stand.

Chapter 12

A New Chapter

November 29th:

Today is the first day of my new career. I have been hired as the Entrepreneurial Services Co-ordinator at Pioneer Technology Center. When I was offered the job the first week of the November, I explained I would like to start at the end of the month, with Thanksgiving coming up and the fact Davina's dad was very sick. I just couldn't start right away. I knew I was going to work for some great people when they said they completely understood what I was going through, and said they just wanted me to start before December 1st. I also said I wanted to start on a Wednesday, and they asked why. I asked if the reason kids coming back to school from summer break usually start on a Thursday is because it is hard for them to focus after being out of school for so long. Of course, both the people who hired me nodded their heads yes. I explained I hadn't worked for almost 18 months. They completely understood what I meant. It was going to be brutal for me to work more than three days the first week. I can tell you it was hard to be in the same place for eight hours but somehow, I made it through.

December 8th – Benji's Facebook post: I wanted to let everyone know that I am now working at Pioneer Technology Center. I am the Entrepreneurial Service Coordinator in the Business and Industry Services area. A large part of my job will be helping startup businesses prepare business plans and financials to make sure they are ready to talk to the bank.

It has been almost 18 months since I have worked and so many of you have been a huge part of me having the attitude that "I can do this." I will never be able to thank you for all the thoughts and prayers, but I will continue to pay it forward. Hopefully with my new job I will be able to be a small part of helping someone to get their dream off the ground and for them to be successful in their new adventure.

Thank you again for all you have done to help Davina and myself, the past year and a half.

I Hope You All Have A Merry Christmas

December 18th – Benji's Facebook post: A year and a half. 18 months. 548 days. I got sick on June 18th, 2016. The doctors told me that the recovery would be 12-18 months. I just shook my head and said to myself that I would be back in a couple months. TOPS! I hate to say it, but they knew what they were saying. The first 6 months (through December) was just trying to make it to the next day because it wasn't a given. The next 3 months (to March) was trying to get enough strength to go and do ANYTHING for more than 5 minutes. April was my chance to really hunt and it was tough going to say the least. 13 months later (July 6th) had my last surgery. 15 months later (September 29th) I had the opportunity to speak at a banquet for the Oklahoma Blood Institute. 17 months later (November 29th) I went to work at a new job.

I am so thankful during this holiday season for all of you that had even the smallest amount of help that you have given me. From the friends and family that gave blood, church fundraiser for medical expenses, bringing Thanksgiving lunch between hospital stays, driving me to surgeries, mowing the yard, taking care of our animals, sending cards or flowers.... The list could go on for days for sure. To each and every person that did anything, please know how much my family appreciates all that you did.

I want to give a special Thank You to every person that PRAYED for us. There is no doubt in my mind that I wouldn't be here if not for that. The power of prayer does work!!!

If you want to give in a way that you never have before, stop by an OBI Blood Drive this holiday season. Is there a better gift than the gift of life? If not for the 42 people that gave blood that I received, you wouldn't be reading this post. There is a big drive at the Cox Center on December 30th. Thunder's cheerleaders, Rumble and a few Thunder players just might be there!!! Swing by and save a life. Remember that this time of year is all about giving and not receiving.

Thanks again for all of your support over the past year. I will be PAYING IT FORWARD and not back because I know that is the best way to help more people.

Remember to be thankful for the trials and tribulations that we all go through. Merry Christmas to everyone and Thanks again

Davina

December 25th – Davina's Facebook post: The miracle of Christmas. Last year we spent our Christmas afternoon in the ER. It wasn't even Benji's worst day;

it had become our lifestyle. He had lost so much weight that he was literally skin on skeleton. That day the pain was more severe than normal. But what I remember was that when we got home, Benji was more like the man I married than the man he had been the past 6 months. He felt well enough to eat & even joke with his family. Once again, hope was born.

I doubt I will ever fully realize the miracle of the original Christmas. But I do know that: LOVE, GRACE, & HOPE ruled the day

Today I stand strong in His promises.

Happy birthday, Jesus. #prayforbenji #humbledby-prayer

***

What Happened?

Benji

As I mentioned in the beginning, I was diagnosed with Type 2 Diabetes in May 2008. I also had high cholesterol and triglycerides at that time. This was diagnosed at an Urgent Care because I hadn't looked for a primary care doctor since moving to Ponca City in July 2007. Once I did find a doctor, he put me on a couple of different medications for the diabetes, cholesterol and triglycerides.

One of the medications I was put on after a couple of years was a new drug to help with diabetes. It is a SGLT2 inhibitor that came out in 2013. These types of pills are for Type 2 diabetics with poorly controlled blood glucose. The list of side effects for the drug included: ketoacidosis, acute kidney injury, pancreatitis, high triglycerides, amputations and even death.

Basically, I managed to go five for six on the major side effects. The FDA required the company to add additional side effects and/or strengthen the warning on their box in May 2015 and June 2016. I am by no means saying this was the cause of my illness, but it could have been a contributing factor. In discussions with my doctors, they can't decide if the pancreatitis, ketoacidosis, or high triglycerides caused the others. It wouldn't surprise me if it was a combination of all of them.

***

Opioids

I feel it is important to talk about the opioids that I was on for almost 18 months. I had never really understood how people could get addicted to pain medication and have so many issues trying to get off them. There is no longer any doubt in my mind that I understand it now. While I was sick, Davina would go to work before I woke up. There were a couple of days one week when I was home between hospital stays (guessing in October) that I just felt horrible when she came home for lunch. I was having cold sweats and was shaking. Not crazy shaking, but I was shaking. After the second time this happened, she asked if I had taken my medicine. I told her I couldn't remember if I had taken them or not. She went back and checked and I hadn't taken them. It was at that time I had a small understanding of what withdrawals were like for people who were addicted. This was *not* a feeling I enjoyed. I have also heard the stories of people that have stolen pills from people that have had surgery, pawned their household goods or stolen things from other people just to be able to buy more pills. I didn't want to become that person.

I had been on IV Fentanyl when I was in the coma, then morphine and oral hydrocodone until September/October, when they changed the morphine to Dilaudid. When they gave me the first dose of Dilaudid, I understood the high that people chase. I did not like that feeling but now I understand why some people might. As the nurse was injecting the Dilaudid, I could feel a warmth go up my arm, across my chest and down to my toes. Then I felt like I was floating a foot off the bed. It only lasted about 20 seconds, but I didn't like it. Luckily, it never made me feel that way again.

During the times I was at home, I was on oral morphine and hydrocodone for a majority of 18 months. In about March of 2017, I told Dr. Gray, my family doctor, I was ready to get off the pills because the pain had finally started to subside. He said that with the surgery coming up to fix my hernia, he would prefer I wait to get off the pills until the surgery was complete, because it is more difficult to come off the pills a second time. He knew that the hernia surgery would be very painful. Once I got over the pain from the hernia surgery, we decided on a plan of action.

It took about six weeks to get off the pain pills. I won't lie; it was a very difficult thing to do. By no means will I say it was easy. It wasn't always good times. But I did it. I knew in my mind that I no longer wanted to take the pills, so I fought through those hard days.

If you know someone with addiction, please don't fight them. Help them by being positive and trying to do anything you can to help them with the addiction and don't put them down, because it isn't easy. Even if you want to get off the drugs, it can be a struggle.

***

Fitting Quote

I recently heard this quote. I am in no way comparing what I went through to the torture he had (at times it may have felt like I was being held hostage), but Admiral James Stockdale said this regarding his time as a POW in Vietnam. It really hit home when I heard it, and I had many of these same feelings at different times during my illness. The quote comes from the Jim Collins book, *Good to Great*, and has been named "The Stockdale Paradox"

> *"I never lost faith in the end of the story. I never doubted not only that I would get out, but also that I would prevail in the end and turn the experience into the defining event of my life, which, in retrospect, I would not trade. You must never confuse faith that you will prevail in the end – which you can never afford to lose – with the discipline to confront the most brutal facts of your current reality, whatever they might be."*[2]

This was me! I had days where everyone wasn't sure I would survive. My faith in God kept me going, and I really don't think I would be here without it. There is no doubt my illness was something I wouldn't want to repeat, but I wouldn't be who I am today if I had not gone through it. I wouldn't want it any other way.

---

[2] J. Collins. (n.d). Excerpts from *Good to Great, The Stockdale paradox*. Retrieved from https://www.jimcollins.com/concepts/Stockdale-Concept.html

***

My Guardian Angel - Aaron

Early on, I mentioned how Aaron pretty much saved my life by bringing me back home from Stillwater when I first didn't feel well. I truly believe he saved my life by bringing me back to Ponca. If I had gone on to Okemah, I more than likely would have ended up in Tulsa, instead of Oklahoma City. This would have been another two hours of driving time for my parents and sister.

In October 2018, I told him to come up and go deer hunting with me. He came up on a Thursday night and we went and checked trail cameras until late in the night. We got up early the next morning and headed to the woods. I gave him directions to his stand and we headed our separate ways. (He couldn't find his stand and blames me for bad directions, but I think he just gets lost easily.) I was able to harvest a deer that morning and we brought it back to the house and started processing the meat. We had fresh venison tenderloin and fried potatoes for lunch. We decided to take a nap before we went back out to the woods. He came and woke me up and we loaded into the truck. We had just left my neighborhood and I noticed I had forgotten my phone. We turned around so I could grab it. I told Aaron I wasn't feeling the best and thought my blood sugar was low, so I asked if he could drive. As we left the neighborhood again, I checked my blood sugar and it was 34. I ate some candy and told him we needed to stop and get a Coke™. As he was driving through town, I started to have a seizure. I was flailing around and banging my head off the truck window. He did a U-turn and drove me to the hospital. When they brought the gurney out, he picked me up by himself and put me directly on it. They wheeled me into the ER and got me hooked up to a glucose IV and got my sugars up. This was the second time he saved my life.

Jodi told me after this episode that Aaron might be a bad luck charm instead of my guardian angel, and maybe I shouldn't hang around with him. I am still not sure if she was joking or being serious. The Motley Crew (Aaron, Bryan and Spencer) joked that she had taken out a one-year restraining order where he couldn't be around me.

In April 2020, I invited Aaron up to go turkey hunting since that year was up. We chased birds all over the property for about four hours, but just couldn't get a bird to come in. After we had been hunting for about three hours, my insulin pump beeped, signaling my sugar was low. I could tell Aaron was nervous about it and was asking how low it was. I told him it was in the high 60's but it wasn't an issue because I had candy to eat. He kept trying to get me to sit down and take a break, so I finally did, just to calm his fears. We sat there for half an hour or so and decided to go to the truck and go, then try our luck at fishing.

Aaron was still concerned, so he decided to get the truck so I wouldn't have to walk as far. While I was sitting there waiting for him to get back, I contemplated setting up my phone to record him coming back, then laying on the ground and acting like I was having another seizure. I didn't end up doing it, but the thought of it had me laughing for days. Aaron said he would have blackened both my eyes if I had done it. I think it would have been worth it! Who needs enemies when you have friends like me? I will never be able to thank him enough for saving my life twice, but there is no doubt I will continue to try.

***

Covid-19

I finished writing this book shortly after the Covid-19 outbreak. I really wish I had been able to finish the book before this. I think it could help some people going through these difficult times. There are millions of people who have been infected with the virus, and more than 100,000 have lost their lives in the United States alone. I hope each person who was in the hospital had half the support network that I had during all of my days in the hospital. I know that most weren't able to have visitors like I was, but faith can take you far. There is no doubt I am living proof of this.

Covid-19 hasn't directly hit my family, but it has affected us, to say the least. My mom woke up March 25th with high blood pressure and was not able to move her left thumb. Dad took her to the emergency room where they found that both carotid arteries were blocked in her neck. One was 90% and the other was 95% blocked. They transferred her to Ft. Worth to a larger hospital. They were able to go in and fix one the next day, and three days later fixed the other one.

The difficult part of that was she had to be in the hospital by herself for about a week. She wasn't able to have that support network that I had. It broke our family's heart to know she was there all alone. Mom was able to go home on March 31st.

On May 17th, my dad woke up early and was having a hard time breathing. Mom took him to the emergency room and he was having a pneumothorax (collapsed lung). He was transferred about 45 miles away to a hospital that had a pulmonologist on staff. He stayed in that hospital for four days, then they transferred him to Ft. Worth to a larger hospital for surgery. So, then my dad was in a hospital with no support network. They scheduled surgery to fix his collapsed lung on Tuesday, May 26th.

During Mom's stay in the hospital, they found a suspicious spot on her lung and they wanted it biopsied. We thought she was having it done on the 26th as well. I decided to make the five-and-a-half-hour drive to Ft. Worth because they would allow one person in with Dad on the day of surgery. We decided it would be best if I was with him and Jodi took Mom to her appointment. I was able to spend all day talking to Dad, which was great, because I hadn't seen him in five months.

When Mom and Jodi got to the hospital, they found out she was just having a Covid-19 test and not the biopsy. She wasn't going to have surgery until the 28th. The issue with this was, Reese, Jodi's daughter and our niece, was having her Sweet 16 birthday party that day at the lake with lots of friends. I decided to stay the whole week and took Mom to her procedure. It was easy and we went home that day, while Dad was still alone in a different hospital.

The results from Mom's biopsy came back as 1st stage cancer. They did a PET scan a couple of weeks later and that was the only piece of cancer they saw, so the doctor scheduled surgery for July 2nd and he expected to be able to go in and take out the cancer and the lymph nodes. Dad was in the waiting room and the doctor came out and told him Mom's cancer was more advanced than expected; there were multiple spots that just didn't show up on the PET scan. He decided it was best to not even take out the piece they originally found. Dad was able to be with her some of the day, but she still had to be by herself for the majority of her stay. She is now home and they will be suggesting a new course of treatments that are very encouraging.

When I was in the hospital my family kept the roads hot by coming to see me. It has been so difficult to *not* be there for my parents when they were always there for me. Parents aren't supposed to have to watch their kids go through life-threatening illnesses. Children are supposed to be there for their parents during their Golden Years and be able to take care of them. The past few months I have not been able to give them the support they gave me. It has been so heartbreaking.

***

Who I Am Today

I am now a blood donor to "pay it forward" for the 42 people who gave me the chance at life. I had to try three times that first week I was allowed to donate. They just couldn't get the blood to flow, but I was determined to give. I had to miss a full year of donations because I traveled out of the country, but I will be reaching a gallon's worth of donations this year. I am really looking forward to this day. I want nothing more than to give someone else that chance at life. The Oklahoma Blood Institute has also developed a program called "Thank the Donor" and I was able to thank all my donors with a message of gratitude. Without the blood I received, it wouldn't matter how hard the doctors worked, I would not have survived.

I am still working at Pioneer Technology Center and getting close to three years on the job. To be honest, it has flown by, looking back at where I was in 2016-2017. I have gained back all the weight I lost (plus some). As a matter of fact, at an appointment with Dr. Kipgen in September 2019, she told me I had gained a few more pounds from my visit four months prior and was up to 225. That day, I happened to ask the receptionist up front what I weighed the first time I saw her. It was 132 pounds. I mentioned to Dr. Kipgen that the first time she met me she wanted me to gain weight. Her response was, the first time I met you, I wasn't sure you were going to make it. You needed to add some weight. You have added enough. It's time to stop." We laughed way too hard at that, but she was correct. I need to be back down to what I weighed, 195 pounds, when all this started. One of the problems with being diabetic is the more carbs you eat, the more insulin you use, the more weight you gain. It is a vicious cycle. Ashley, my trainer for my insulin pump, has also been so helpful in explaining everything about the pump. She even put supplies in her mailbox for me to pick up one time when I was traveling and forgot to bring them. Thank you, Ashley, for being so kind and helpful!

I am still enjoying my time in the outdoors. I never take for granted any minute that I spend outside in nature. I have spoken to God many more times while in a tree-stand since that day. Every time I walk up to an animal that I have harvested; I thank HIM for the opportunity to put food on the table and giving me many more days to watch the sun rise in the morning and set in the evening. HIS miracles never cease to amaze me. Our God is an Awesome God!!! All throughout my illness and too this day Davina will just say "But God..." It always brings a smile to my face.

One "positive" that came out of my illness is how close I have become with my sister. For many years, we would only talk on the phone when something big happened, like nephew hit a home run; niece set a school record in track. Mother's Day or Father's Day is coming up and what should we get Mom and Dad. We would text back and forth on occasion, but we seldom just called to talk. I have never been a huge fan of talking on the phone, but we talked almost every day while I was sick. It was usually about how I was feeling, but sometimes we would just talk about nothing. Kind of like a Seinfeld episode. It isn't that we didn't love each other, but we weren't as close as some siblings. This definitely did bring us closer together. We don't talk every day now, but it is still more often than it used to be.

Davina and I are celebrating our seventh year of marriage this year. We have added another Golden Retriever, Bear, to our list of pets. He is a Bear, to say the least. We have had a chance to take some trips and life is as normal as it will ever be for us; I am *not* saying that's a bad thing.

I will be on insulin and other medications the rest of my life. Since my pancreas is basically gone, the medicine keeps me alive. If all I need to do to live another day, week, month, year, or decade is take a handful of pills a day, I will take it.

Life is worth living when you have the family and friends that I have. I am blessed with more than I deserve in that regard and for that I am grateful.

BUT GOD!

ABOUT
KHARIS PUBLISHING

KHARIS PUBLISHING is an independent, traditional publishing house with a core mission to publish impactful books, and channel proceeds into establishing mini-libraries or resource centers for orphanages in developing countries, so these kids will learn to read, dream, and grow. Every time you purchase a book from Kharis Publishing or partner as an author, you are helping give these kids an amazing opportunity to read, dream, and grow. Kharis Publishing is an imprint of Kharis Media LLC. Learn more at https://www.kharispublishing.com.

CPSIA information can be obtained
at www.ICGtesting.com
Printed in the USA
FSHW020801110321
79284FS